WILLY BRANDT

WILLY BRANDT

Tom Viola

CHELSEA HOUSE PUBLISHERS
NEW YORK
NEW HAVEN   PHILADELPHIA

EDITOR-IN-CHIEF: Nancy Toff
EXECUTIVE EDITOR: Remmel T. Nunn
MANAGING EDITOR: Karyn Gullen Browne
COPY CHIEF: Juliann Barbato
PICTURE EDITOR: Adrian G. Allen
ART DIRECTOR: Giannella Garrett
MANUFACTURING MANAGER: Gerald Levine

Staff for WILLY BRANDT:

SENIOR EDITOR: John W. Selfridge
ASSISTANT EDITOR: Bert Yaeger
COPY EDITOR: Terrance Dolan
EDITORIAL ASSISTANT: Scott Ash
ASSOCIATE PICTURE EDITOR: Juliette Dickstein
PICTURE RESEARCHER: Alan Gottlieb
SENIOR DESIGNER: David Murray
ASSISTANT DESIGNER: Jill Goldreyer
DESIGNERS: Laura Lang, Donna Sinisgalli
PRODUCTION COORDINATOR: Joseph Romano
COVER ILLUSTRATION: Kye Carbone

CREATIVE DIRECTOR: Harold Steinberg

3 5 7 9 8 6 4 2

Library of Congress Cataloging in Publication Data

Viola, Tom. WILLY BRANDT

(World leaders past & present)
Bibliography: p.
Includes index.
1. Brandt, Willy, 1913– , —Juvenile literature. 2. Heads of
state—Germany (West)—Biography—Juvenile literature. 3.
Germany (West)—Politics and government—Juvenile literature.
[1. Brandt, Willy, 1913– . 2. Heads of State] I. Title. II. Series.
DD260.8.V56 1988   943.087′092′4 [B] [92]
87-14685
ISBN 0-87754-512-X

Contents

JOHN ADAMS
JOHN QUINCY ADAMS
KONRAD ADENAUER
ALEXANDER THE GREAT
SALVADOR ALLENDE
MARC ANTONY
CORAZON AQUINO
YASIR ARAFAT
KING ARTHUR
HAFEZ AL-ASSAD
KEMAL ATATÜRK
ATTILA
CLEMENT ATTLEE
AUGUSTUS CAESAR
MENACHEM BEGIN
DAVID BEN-GURION
OTTO VON BISMARCK
LÉON BLUM
SIMON BOLÍVAR
CESARE BORGIA
WILLY BRANDT
LEONID BREZHNEV
JULIUS CAESAR
JOHN CALVIN
JIMMY CARTER
FIDEL CASTRO
CATHERINE THE GREAT
CHARLEMAGNE
CHIANG KAI-SHEK
WINSTON CHURCHILL
GEORGES CLEMENCEAU
CLEOPATRA
CONSTANTINE THE GREAT
HERNÁN CORTÉS
OLIVER CROMWELL
GEORGES-JACQUES
    DANTON
JEFFERSON DAVIS
MOSHE DAYAN
CHARLES DE GAULLE
EAMON DE VALERA
EUGENE DEBS
DENG XIAOPING
BENJAMIN DISRAELI
ALEXANDER DUBČEK
FRANÇOIS & JEAN-CLAUDE
    DUVALIER
DWIGHT EISENHOWER
ELEANOR OF AQUITAINE
ELIZABETH I
FAISAL
FERDINAND & ISABELLA
FRANCISCO FRANCO
BENJAMIN FRANKLIN

FREDERICK THE GREAT
INDIRA GANDHI
MOHANDAS GANDHI
GIUSEPPE GARIBALDI
AMIN & BASHIR GEMAYEL
GENGHIS KHAN
WILLIAM GLADSTONE
MIKHAIL GORBACHEV
ULYSSES S. GRANT
ERNESTO "CHE" GUEVARA
TENZIN GYATSO
ALEXANDER HAMILTON
DAG HAMMARSKJÖLD
HENRY VIII
HENRY OF NAVARRE
PAUL VON HINDENBURG
HIROHITO
ADOLF HITLER
HO CHI MINH
KING HUSSEIN
IVAN THE TERRIBLE
ANDREW JACKSON
JAMES I
WOJCIECH JARUZELSKI
THOMAS JEFFERSON
JOAN OF ARC
POPE JOHN XXIII
POPE JOHN PAUL II
LYNDON JOHNSON
BENITO JUÁREZ
JOHN KENNEDY
ROBERT KENNEDY
JOMO KENYATTA
AYATOLLAH KHOMEINI
NIKITA KHRUSHCHEV
KIM IL SUNG
MARTIN LUTHER KING, JR.
HENRY KISSINGER
KUBLAI KHAN
LAFAYETTE
ROBERT E. LEE
VLADIMIR LENIN
ABRAHAM LINCOLN
DAVID LLOYD GEORGE
LOUIS XIV
MARTIN LUTHER
JUDAS MACCABEUS
JAMES MADISON
NELSON & WINNIE
    MANDELA
MAO ZEDONG
FERDINAND MARCOS
GEORGE MARSHALL

MARY, QUEEN OF SCOTS
TOMÁŠ MASARYK
GOLDA MEIR
KLEMENS VON METTERNICH
JAMES MONROE
HOSNI MUBARAK
ROBERT MUGABE
BENITO MUSSOLINI
NAPOLÉON BONAPARTE
GAMAL ABDEL NASSER
JAWAHARLAL NEHRU
NERO
NICHOLAS II
RICHARD NIXON
KWAME NKRUMAH
DANIEL ORTEGA
MOHAMMED REZA PAHLAVI
THOMAS PAINE
CHARLES STEWART
    PARNELL
PERICLES
JUAN PERÓN
PETER THE GREAT
POL POT
MUAMMAR EL-QADDAFI
RONALD REAGAN
CARDINAL RICHELIEU
MAXIMILIEN ROBESPIERRE
ELEANOR ROOSEVELT
FRANKLIN ROOSEVELT
THEODORE ROOSEVELT
ANWAR SADAT
HAILE SELASSIE
PRINCE SIHANOUK
JAN SMUTS
JOSEPH STALIN
SUKARNO
SUN YAT-SEN
TAMERLANE
MOTHER TERESA
MARGARET THATCHER
JOSIP BROZ TITO
TOUSSAINT L'OUVERTURE
LEON TROTSKY
PIERRE TRUDEAU
HARRY TRUMAN
QUEEN VICTORIA
LECH WALESA
GEORGE WASHINGTON
CHAIM WEIZMANN
WOODROW WILSON
XERXES
EMILIANO ZAPATA
ZHOU ENLAI

CHELSEA HOUSE PUBLISHERS

ON LEADERSHIP

Arthur M. Schlesinger, jr.

LEADERSHIP, it may be said, is really what makes the world go round. Love no doubt smooths the passage; but love is a private transaction between consenting adults. Leadership is a public transaction with history. The idea of leadership affirms the capacity of individuals to move, inspire, and mobilize masses of people so that they act together in pursuit of an end. Sometimes leadership serves good purposes, sometimes bad; but whether the end is benign or evil, great leaders are those men and women who leave their personal stamp on history.

Now, the very concept of leadership implies the proposition that individuals can make a difference. This proposition has never been universally accepted. From classical times to the present day, eminent thinkers have regarded individuals as no more than the agents and pawns of larger forces, whether the gods and goddesses of the ancient world or, in the modern era, race, class, nation, the dialectic, the will of the people, the spirit of the times, history itself. Against such forces, the individual dwindles into insignificance.

So contends the thesis of historical determinism. Tolstoy's great novel *War and Peace* offers a famous statement of the case. Why, Tolstoy asked, did millions of men in the Napoleonic Wars, denying their human feelings and their common sense, move back and forth across Europe slaughtering their fellows? "The war," Tolstoy answered, "was bound to happen simply because it was bound to happen." All prior history predetermined it. As for leaders, they, Tolstoy said, "are but the labels that serve to give a name to an end and, like labels, they have the least possible connection with the event." The greater the leader, "the more conspicuous the inevitability and the predestination of every act he commits." The leader, said Tolstoy, is "the slave of history."

Determinism takes many forms. Marxism is the determinism of class. Nazism the determinism of race. But the idea of men and women as the slaves of history runs athwart the deepest human instincts. Rigid determinism abolishes the idea of human freedom—

the assumption of free choice that underlies every move we make, every word we speak, every thought we think. It abolishes the idea of human responsibility, since it is manifestly unfair to reward or punish people for actions that are by definition beyond their control. No one can live consistently by any deterministic creed. The Marxist states prove this themselves by their extreme susceptibility to the cult of leadership.

More than that, history refutes the idea that individuals make no difference. In December 1931 a British politician crossing Park Avenue in New York City between 76th and 77th Streets around 10:30 P.M. looked in the wrong direction and was knocked down by an automobile—a moment, he later recalled, of a man aghast, a world aglare: "I do not understand why I was not broken like an eggshell or squashed like a gooseberry." Fourteen months later an American politician, sitting in an open car in Miami, Florida, was fired on by an assassin; the man beside him was hit. Those who believe that individuals make no difference to history might well ponder whether the next two decades would have been the same had Mario Constasino's car killed Winston Churchill in 1931 and Giuseppe Zangara's bullet killed Franklin Roosevelt in 1933. Suppose, in addition, that Adolf Hitler had been killed in the street fighting during the Munich *Putsch* of 1923 and that Lenin had died of typhus during World War I. What would the 20th century be like now?

For better or for worse, individuals do make a difference. "The notion that a people can run itself and its affairs anonymously," wrote the philosopher William James, "is now well known to be the silliest of absurdities. Mankind does nothing save through initiatives on the part of inventors, great or small, and imitation by the rest of us—these are the sole factors in human progress. Individuals of genius show the way, and set the patterns, which common people then adopt and follow."

Leadership, James suggests, means leadership in thought as well as in action. In the long run, leaders in thought may well make the greater difference to the world. But, as Woodrow Wilson once said, "Those only are leaders of men, in the general eye, who lead in action. . . . It is at their hands that new thought gets its translation into the crude language of deeds." Leaders in thought often invent in solitude and obscurity, leaving to later generations the tasks of imitation. Leaders in action—the leaders portrayed in this series—have to be effective in their own time.

And they cannot be effective by themselves. They must act in response to the rhythms of their age. Their genius must be adapted, in a phrase of William James's, "to the receptivities of the moment." Leaders are useless without followers. "There goes the mob," said the French politician hearing a clamor in the streets. "I am their leader. I must follow them." Great leaders turn the inchoate emotions of the mob to purposes of their own. They seize on the opportunities of their time, the hopes, fears, frustrations, crises, potentialities. They succeed when events have prepared the way for them, when the community is awaiting to be aroused, when they can provide the clarifying and organizing ideas. Leadership ignites the circuit between the individual and the mass and thereby alters history.

It may alter history for better or for worse. Leaders have been responsible for the most extravagant follies and most monstrous crimes that have beset suffering humanity. They have also been vital in such gains as humanity has made in individual freedom, religious and racial tolerance, social justice, and respect for human rights.

There is no sure way to tell in advance who is going to lead for good and who for evil. But a glance at the gallery of men and women in *World Leaders—Past and Present* suggests some useful tests.

One test is this: Do leaders lead by force or by persuasion? By command or by consent? Through most of history leadership was exercised by the divine right of authority. The duty of followers was to defer and to obey. "Theirs not to reason why / Theirs but to do and die." On occasion, as with the so-called enlightened despots of the 18th century in Europe, absolutist leadership was animated by humane purposes. More often, absolutism nourished the passion for domination, land, gold, and conquest and resulted in tyranny.

The great revolution of modern times has been the revolution of equality. The idea that all people should be equal in their legal condition has undermined the old structure of authority, hierarchy, and deference. The revolution of equality has had two contrary effects on the nature of leadership. For equality, as Alexis de Tocqueville pointed out in his great study *Democracy in America*, might mean equality in servitude as well as equality in freedom.

"I know of only two methods of establishing equality in the political world," Tocqueville wrote. "Rights must be given to every citizen, or none at all to anyone . . . save one, who is the master of all." There was no middle ground "between the sovereignty of all and the absolute power of one man." In his astonishing prediction of 20th-century totalitarian dictatorship, Tocqueville explained how the revolution of equality could lead to the *"Führerprinzip"* and more terrible absolutism than the world had ever known.

But when rights are given to every citizen and the sovereignty of all is established, the problem of leadership takes a new form, becomes more exacting than ever before. It is easy to issue commands and enforce them by the rope and the stake, the concentration camp and the *gulag.* It is much harder to use argument and achievement to overcome opposition and win consent. The Founding Fathers of the United States understood the difficulty. They believed that history had given them the opportunity to decide, as Alexander Hamilton wrote in the first Federalist Paper, whether men are indeed capable of basing government on "reflection and choice, or whether they are forever destined to depend . . . on accident and force."

Government by reflection and choice called for a new style of leadership and a new quality of followership. It required leaders to be responsive to popular concerns, and it required followers to be active and informed participants in the process. Democracy does not eliminate emotion from politics; sometimes it fosters demagoguery; but it is confident that, as the greatest of democratic leaders put it, you cannot fool all of the people all of the time. It measures leadership by results and retires those who overreach or falter or fail.

It is true that in the long run despots are measured by results too. But they can postpone the day of judgment, sometimes indefinitely, and in the meantime they can do infinite harm. It is also true that democracy is no guarantee of virtue and intelligence in government, for the voice of the people is not necessarily the voice of God. But democracy, by assuring the right of opposition, offers built-in resistance to the evils inherent in absolutism. As the theologian Reinhold Niebuhr summed it up, "Man's capacity for justice makes democracy possible, but man's inclination to injustice makes democracy necessary."

A second test for leadership is the end for which power is sought. When leaders have as their goal the supremacy of a master race or the promotion of totalitarian revolution or the acquisition and exploitation of colonies or the protection of greed and privilege or the preservation of personal power, it is likely that their leadership will do little to advance the cause of humanity. When their goal is the abolition of slavery, the liberation of women, the enlargement of opportunity for the poor and powerless, the extension of equal rights to racial minorities, the defense of the freedoms of expression and opposition, it is likely that their leadership will increase the sum of human liberty and welfare.

Leaders have done great harm to the world. They have also conferred great benefits. You will find both sorts in this series. Even "good" leaders must be regarded with a certain wariness. Leaders are not demigods; they put on their trousers one leg after another just like ordinary mortals. No leader is infallible, and every leader needs to be reminded of this at regular intervals. Irreverence irritates leaders but is their salvation. Unquestioning submission corrupts leaders and demeans followers. Making a cult of a leader is always a mistake. Fortunately hero worship generates its own antidote. "Every hero," said Emerson, "becomes a bore at last."

The signal benefit the great leaders confer is to embolden the rest of us to live according to our own best selves, to be active, insistent, and resolute in affirming our own sense of things. For great leaders attest to the reality of human freedom against the supposed inevitabilities of history. And they attest to the wisdom and power that may lie within the most unlikely of us, which is why Abraham Lincoln remains the supreme example of great leadership. A great leader, said Emerson, exhibits new possibilities to all humanity. "We feed on genius. . . . Great men exist that there may be greater men."

Great leaders, in short, justify themselves by emancipating and empowering their followers. So humanity struggles to master its destiny, remembering with Alexis de Tocqueville: "It is true that around every man a fatal circle is traced beyond which he cannot pass; but within the wide verge of that circle he is powerful and free; as it is with man, so with communities."

1

Flight from the Nazis

On the afternoon of February 19, 1933, a bitter cold wind howled through the German port city of Lübeck on the Baltic Sea. Despite the icy temperatures, a crowd of 15,000 people gathered on the Burgfeld — a parade ground in the center of town — to protest the policies of the three-week-old government of Chancellor Adolf Hitler.

Hitler's official decree banning all labor union strikes had sparked the protest. It was the most powerful demonstration the city had ever witnessed. But for 19-year-old Herbert Frahm — to be better known in the future as Willy Brandt — this was an event that heralded great changes in his life as well as in the course of history.

This rally held particular significance for young Frahm, for it featured an appearance by Dr. Julius Leber. As a prominent member of the Social Democratic party, or SPD, Leber was an outspoken opponent of Hitler's National Socialist German Workers' party (or NSDAP), better known as the *Nazis*.

During the German economic crisis of the early 1920s, a woman lights her stove using millions in almost worthless German currency, then called *reichsmarks*. By 1923 reparations payments owed by Germany to the Allied victors of World War I had caused inflation so severe that 4 billion marks were equal to a single U.S. dollar.

Dr. Julius Leber, the Social Democratic party (SPD), organizer and editor of the newspaper *Volksbote*, in 1930. A representative to the *Reichstag*, or parliament, Leber encouraged young Herbert Frahm's journalistic abilities.

A tall, hot-tempered young man, Frahm was outspoken and assertive, and Leber recognized that the youth would be invaluable to the Social Democrats in their continuing struggle with the Nazis. Leber offered Frahm a job with the Social Democratic newspaper *Volksbote* (*The People Speak*), and soon thereafter sponsored him for membership in the Social Democratic party.

"Willy Brandt," as his readers knew him, was a good reporter. Under Leber's guidance he became confident as a journalist and one of the most promising young members of the Social Democratic organization. But the Social Democrats were on the defensive. By the early 1930s, the worldwide Great Depression had crippled the German economy. Millions were unemployed and German currency had become practically worthless. The prices of everyday necessities — food and clothing, soap, shoes — rose meteorically as jobs became increasingly difficult to find. Germany had not fully recovered from the disastrous defeat of World War I, and the German people were angry and frustrated with the peace terms imposed by the victorious Allies in the Treaty of Versailles, signed in June 1919. Many Germans found the terms of the Treaty of Versailles harsh and humiliating.

The Weimar republic, a democratic government established in Germany immediately after World War I to replace the defeated monarchy, was unpopular with many Germans and faced impossible odds. The domestic political chaos that ensued was aggravated by a disastrous inflation that impoverished much of the middle class. In addition, the German Communist party and the extreme right-wing Nazi party were in bitter and violent opposition to one another. These two parties battled each other in Germany's streets over who would do away with the Weimar republic. Both were discontented with the democratic coalition government. While able statesmen such as Gustav Stresemann and the Republic's first president Friedrich Ebert (1919–1925), struggled to keep the government standing, it could not long endure opposition from both the extreme Left and Right.

Adolf Hitler was a fanatical German nationalist who played upon German discontent by denouncing the Treaty of Versailles. As his popularity grew among Germans exhausted by defeat and despair, his ferocity intensified. It was not long before he was denouncing not only the treaty and the foreign powers that had defeated Germany, but also Jewish citizens, leftist politicians, and finally, anyone who was not a Nazi. In radio addresses and at public rallies Hitler promised to create a prosperous and glorified Germany and aroused millions with a frenzied nationalist rhetoric. Soon Hitler demanded that he be named chancellor.

On January 30, 1933, Hitler was finally appointed chancellor of the German republic by President Paul von Hindenburg. The man who wanted to make himself Germany's absolute dictator wasted no time in securing his position and the grip of the Nazi party on Germany. Political opponents were beaten and arrested. Others simply disappeared. Two days after Hitler's rise to power, Julius Leber was accosted by a band of the Nazi's paramilitary storm troopers; the Stürmabteilung, or SA. Insults were exchanged. In the brawl that followed, Leber was severely injured and carried home unconscious. Hours later, members of Hitler's secret police, the *Gestapo*, a shortened form for *Geheimnis Staatspolizei*, awoke Leber's household to charge him with assault. Although it seemed clear that he had been provoked and only acted in self-defense, Leber was arrested on the spot and taken to prison.

Nazi storm troopers, members of the *Stürmabteilung*, or S.A., hold members of the Social Democratic and the Catholic Center parties at gunpoint. After Adolf Hitler became chancellor of Germany in January 1933, he outlawed all parties except his own National Socialist German Workers' (Nazi) party.

People in Lübeck were outraged. Despite government warnings that the recent order from the chancellor's office officially prohibiting any labor union to call a strike would be strictly enforced, Lübeck's workers, including sailors, longshoremen, and fishermen, defied Hitler and demanded a work stoppage to call for Leber's immediate release. Union leadership, however, frightened by the growing power and unchecked brutality of Hitler's Gestapo, refused to go against the government by authorizing a strike.

The refusal of union leadership to resist the Nazis' blatant attempt to control the unions spread fury through Lübeck. Fearing that Leber might not survive in prison, Frahm, as "Willy Brandt," hastily abandoned his newspaper work to devote all his energies to organizing the strike.

For two weeks the Nazi government and the workers were at an impasse, each waiting for the other to back down. Finally, a compromise was reached. A brief, one-hour protest strike would be permitted. Hitler's government hoped that Lübeck would be intimidated by the possibility of violence and choose to ignore the protest, thus giving the Nazis a decided psychological victory.

Trade unionists gather outside their union hall in Lübeck in 1933, the year Hitler became chancellor. Workers like Brandt's grandfather Ludwig Frahm, had long made the Social Democrats the leading party in Lübeck, and even after Hitler's rise to power, the party remained popular there.

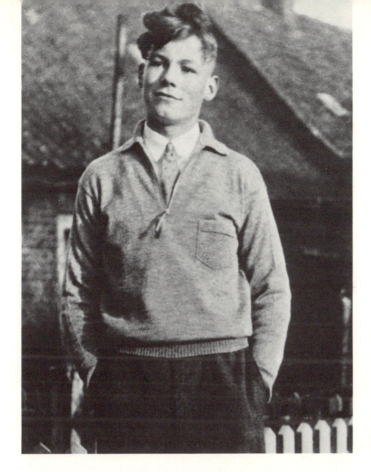

The year before Nazi dictatorship ended Germany's short-lived democratic government (created in 1919), Willy Brandt was already a political firebrand. He was raised by his mother and his grandfather, a loyal Social Democrat.

Leber's wife, meanwhile, successfully negotiated a short-term release for her husband. In an attempt to appear benevolent and ease political tension, the Nazis even agreed to allow Leber to appear at the rally under one strict stipulation: he was forbidden to speak. Allowing Leber to appear in public, the Nazis reasoned, would put an end to the protest, keep a political enemy from becoming a martyr, and quiet demands for his permanent release until opposition could be silenced for good.

Just as the freezing wind whipping off the Baltic did not discourage them from coming to the rally, these workers of Lübeck could not be frightened away by the Nazis' threats. On the day of the protest, Herbert Frahm stood among thousands who waited for sight of Leber on the hastily constructed platform at the far end of the common. As numerous representatives of the striking workers spoke, Nazi storm troopers walked through the crowd intimidating those they could with a bump or shove.

17

The principal leaders of the Allied nations meet in June 1919 in Versailles, France (left to right): British prime minister David Lloyd George, Italian prime minister Vittorio Orlando, French premier Georges Clemenceau, and U.S. president Woodrow Wilson. With the resulting Treaty of Versailles, the Allies dissolved the German Empire and demanded huge payments for damages.

A hush fell over the crowd as Leber appeared at the edge of the stage. Even from far away, Frahm could see that Leber had been badly beaten; his face was swollen and bruised. As he slowly walked to center stage, Leber angrily refused assistance from a Nazi official. It was evident to all that every step caused him great pain. Seeing this, Frahm felt his heart pound faster and faster until it seemed his chest would explode. Just when it seemed neither Frahm nor those around him could bear the silence a moment longer, Leber threw his arms into the air and shouted a single word: *"Freiheit!"* ("Freedom!")

This word shattered the silence and rang through the frigid winter wind. Men and women broke into cheers, echoing the call and pounding their feet on the frozen ground. Shouting this single word again and again, their voices rose as if the wind could carry their response to Hitler and his government in Berlin.

In the excitement few noticed as Leber was taken from the stage by Hitler's agents. Frahm had not taken his eyes off Leber from the moment he stepped into view. Now, seeing him rushed off the platform, Frahm angrily shoved through the crowd to get to the stage. But he could not move through the masses fast enough. Leber was gone, a prisoner of the Nazi regime.

European Boundaries After World War I—1919

ESTONIA

LATVIA

LITHUANIA

WHITE (NONCOMMUNIST) RUSSIA

DENMARK

Baltic Sea

NETHERLANDS

Kiel
Lübeck
Hamburg
Bremen

GERMANY (WEIMAR REPUBLIC)

Berlin

Oder River

POLAND

Warsaw

Elbe River

Breslau

Paris

Rhine River

Nuremberg (Nürnberg)

CZECHOSLOVAKIA

GALATIA

RUTHENIA

BESSARABIA

SWITZERLAND

Vienna

AUSTRIA-HUNGARY

ROMANIA

FRANCE

YUGOSLAVIA

SERBIA

Danube River

BOSNIA

BULGARIA

ITALY

Adriatic Sea

Rome

Mediterranean Sea

ceded by Germany after Allied Victory in 1918		ceded by Bulgaria	
ceded by Austria-Hungary after Allied Victory		Allied-occupied Rhineland	
ceded by Russia		Territories kept or ceded according to Plebiscites conducted by League of Nations 1920–1922	

•••••••••••• 1914 Boundaries   - - - - - - 1926 Boundaries

After Germany surrendered to the Allies on November 11, 1918, French armies occupied the German Rhineland. France also recovered Alsace and Lorraine, lost to the Germans in 1870. Allied occupation of the Rhineland ended in the mid-1930s. Although intended as a demilitarized zone, the Rhineland was occupied by German troops in 1936.

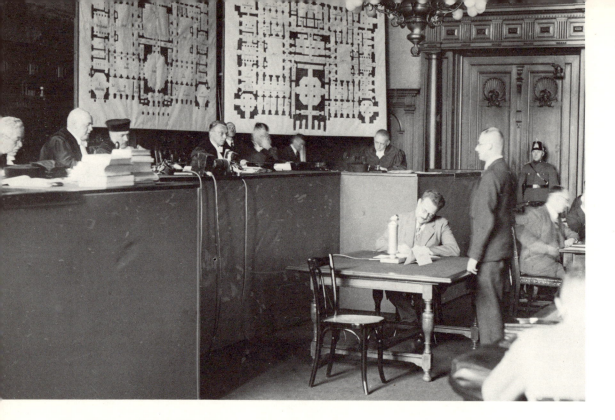

In 1934 a communist was tried and convicted of setting fire to the Reichstag building in Berlin. The fire was used by Chancellor Hitler to persuade President Paul von Hindenburg to suspend civil liberties and parts of the Weimar Constitution.

Four days after the rally in Lübeck, those remaining in government who were courageous enough to oppose Hitler were delivered a decisive blow. On February 23, a fire broke out in the building where the *Reichstag*, or parliament, held its sessions. This suspicious event played straight into Hitler's hands. He managed to persuade Hindenburg that only if given absolute "emergency powers" could he properly deal with the threat posed by the incident. Communists, Hitler claimed, were to blame for the fire, although it was generally considered more probable that it was set by the Nazis themselves. Calling the fire a prelude to a "bloody uprising and civil war," Hitler promised to have no mercy on those responsible. "The German people will not put up with leniency," he warned the following day. The embers of the Reichstag were barely cold when Hitler outlawed the Social Democratic party and any other political organization that opposed the Nazis.

On March 23, the Reichstag passed the "Enabling Act," effectively stripping itself of all power and firmly establishing Adolf Hitler as dictator. He became Nazi Germany's absolute leader—*der Führer.*

No prominent Social Democrat was safe any longer in Lübeck. For a short while, Frahm and many other party members hid in Berlin's political underground. Days were filled with the news of arrests and missing friends, and rumors of torture and murder. Several of Frahm's young colleagues were seized en route to Berlin and executed. The brutality that swept through Germany was unlike anything Frahm had ever experienced or even imagined. Under Hitler, his homeland had become enemy territory.

In the meantime, secret preparations were made by Social Democratic leaders to base a resistance movement in Oslo, the capital of Norway. The first attempt to get a member of the resistance to Norway ended in arrest. Frahm was the next to attempt this vitally important mission. Eager for what seemed a great adventure, young Frahm readily agreed to attempt an escape to Norway. The enthusiasm he showed toward this mission concealed his unspoken realization that remaining in Germany was now

Soldiers of the Weimar republic's drastically reduced postwar army take aim with a mock antiaircraft gun. The victorious Allies were suspicious of possible German rearmament. By January 1927 an Allied commission concluded that the Germans "never had the intention of disarming."

impossible. His articles in *Volksbote* and his close association with Leber had brought him to the deadly attention of the fearsome Gestapo. To stay would mean certain arrest.

Returning from Berlin to Lübeck, Frahm quickly finalized plans for his escape. Through a trusted friend who worked on the docks, Frahm made contact with a fisherman, Paul Stooss, who would take him across the Baltic Sea to a tiny port called Rødbyhaven on the Danish island of Lolland. From there he could travel freely to Oslo.

The 20-year-old Frahm quietly dropped out of sight, hiding at the fisherman's house until he could set sail for freedom. The escape began smoothly, initial plans falling into place in spite of the dangers. On the evening before he was to slip out of Germany, Frahm stopped on a whim with Stooss in an out-of-the-way pub in a town outside Lübeck. There, Frahm spotted a former comrade who was rumored to have secretly joined the Nazis. His old friend looked up and their eyes locked across the damp wooden bar. Frahm froze with fear. If he left too quickly, he might arouse suspicion and be followed. He would have to stay and behave naturally. Frahm walked over to his old friend, warmly greeting him.

Minutes passed in anguish for Frahm as he drank his beer and made friendly conversation. Convinced that he had given the impression that his presence in the bar was nothing unusual, Frahm said goodbye and left. With Stooss not far behind, he returned to the fisherman's home. As he put on warmer clothing for his voyage, Frahm wondered if his friend, who had once been an enthusiastic member of the Social Democrats, was now reporting him to the Gestapo.

There was not another moment to lose. Boarding Stooss's small boat, a rusting cutter equipped with both a motor and sails, Frahm searched for a hiding place and found a concealed spot behind a stack of heavy wooden crates. There he sat for hours, as the sea air covered everything in a damp and chilling mist.

The 19th-century German philosopher Karl Marx founded modern socialism with Friedrich Engels. Marx, who believed that capitalist societies would be overthrown by the working class, wrote *Das Kapital* (*Capital*), which Brandt studied during his youth.

At dawn, Stooss slipped out of port, sailing past the customs inspectors under cover of a thick gray haze that blocked out the sun. Farther out to sea, Stooss turned on the ship's small engines just as a storm suddenly appeared and began to toss the boat mercilessly. The hours dragged by, and Frahm became violently seasick. He said nothing, however, and waited out the storm, hoping the steady popping of the motor and the rain splattering upon the tarpaulin over his head would lull him to sleep. All that he had brought with him from Germany was this hope, a briefcase filled with 100 *reichsmarks* (the German currency at the time), and a copy of *Das Kapital* (*Capital*), by the 19th-century German philosopher and social theorist Karl Marx. For now, Lübeck was far behind him.

By the time the storm subsided and they arrived at Lolland, Frahm was so ill he could barely stand. He would remain in exile for the next 10 years, waiting for the day when he could return to a Germany that was free from Nazi oppression.

2
Grandfather and Grandson

Herbert Ernst Karl Frahm was born on December 18, 1913, in the German port city of Lübeck. Lübeck was a proud city, once regarded as the queen of the German ports on the Baltic Sea, and the northern gateway to Germany and the European continent. The city had been a bustling center of commerce for more than 500 years.

By 1913, however, Lübeck's luster and vitality had dimmed considerably as the city found itself competing with other port cities, such as Hamburg and Bremen, which were better able to accommodate modern shipping. What remained undimmed in Lübeck, however, was its pride and a centuries-old class system based on the boundaries of the ancient city walls. To be born inside these walls, within the shadows of the medieval Gothic towers and ornate façades of the homes of Lübeck's early ruling families, was to belong to the upper class and to enjoy the advantages that come with such elevated social status.

Like many children whose families were active in the Social Democratic party, Brandt was introduced to politics through the party's youth organizations. Influenced by his grandfather, Brandt first became a member of *Kinderfreunde* (Children's Friends), and by age 18 was a leader in the Socialist Worker Youth.

Herbert Frahm was born in the small, two-bedroom apartment where his grandfather, Ludwig Frahm, lived — well outside the socially respectable part of town. His mother, Martha Frahm, was just 19 when Herbert was born. Herbert never knew his father, who disappeared from Lübeck shortly before his son's birth, bringing considerable disgrace to the Frahm family by his refusal to marry Herbert's mother. Herbert was christened with his mother's family name. His father was never again mentioned in the tiny Frahm household, neither by Martha, who struggled to raise her infant son, nor by Herbert's grandfather, who maintained an icy silence if someone rudely brought up the subject.

Martha worked hard to support herself and her young son. She asked nothing from the boy's grandfather except that he allow her and her son to share the roof over their heads, and that he watch the child while she was away. But in August 1914 World War I began. Archduke Franz Ferdinand's assassination set off a diplomatic war between the German

Empire, Austria-Hungary, and Turkey (the Central Powers), and the Allied forces: France, Great Britain, Tsarist Russia, and the United States. Soon, like every able-bodied man in Germany — almost regardless of age — Herbert's grandfather was drafted into the army. With his grandfather gone, little Herbert was cared for by a neighbor while his mother continued to work at the local market six days a week. As she stocked shelves and packed shopping bags, Martha looked forward to Sundays when she could spend all day with her son and buy him treats from the store. But even these occasional sweets and fruits became scarce as the war dragged on and drained Germany of its resources. Despite hardships, Herbert grew to be a healthy boy.

When Herbert was five years old his grandfather returned to Lübeck from the war. Although well into his 60s, Frahm was a robust and imposing presence in the household. He was also an avid storyteller. Retired from his job as a dockworker, the old man could devote his time to looking after his grandson. When the morning chill had lifted, and after his mother had gone to work, young Herbert would accompany his grandfather on long walks along Lübeck's harbor. There, amid the loud shouts of fishermen unloading the day's haul of herring, and longshoremen stacking rough wooden crates into waiting freighters, Ludwig would introduce his grandson to his old dockmates and spend the rest of the afternoon pointing out the ships and spinning tales of his days on the docks. To Herbert, his grandfather was not an old man reliving the past. His grandfather was a hero.

In truth, Ludwig Frahm was originally one of many thousands of German farm laborers who in the late 19th century came to cities such as Lübeck looking for work. The feudal system of serfdom, whereby the peasants were the property of their masters along with the land, ceased in Germany in 1820. The gradual breakup of many vast family-owned estates left thousands of farm laborers without homes and jobs. Germany's ports and factories offered work in the cities to many who were forced

Young Willy Brandt was an extremely bright student. Despite his impressive school record, however, he decided not to attend a university and chose instead to become an apprentice with a shipping firm.

Karl Liebknecht established the revolutionary Spartacist League and was assassinated by government troops in 1919. His father, the socialist Wilhelm Liebknecht, cofounded the Social Democratic party in 1875.

to turn their backs on farming. The steady arrival of the urban working class transformed many of Germany's cities into centers of manufacturing and commerce. Lübeck was one such city. As the ranks of the urban working class grew, a new political organization came into being: the Social Democratic party. Initially, the Social Democrats were made up entirely of this growing segment of the population.

The Social Democratic party was established by followers of the famed socialist thinkers Karl Marx and Friedrich Engels, who claimed that conflict between workers and capitalists would end with the overthrow of capitalism, the system of private ownership. They believed that a society without classes would emerge in its place. Founded by August Bebel and socialist Wilhelm Liebknecht in 1875, the Social Democrats became Germany's largest political party by 1912 — two years before the outbreak of World War I. These socialists believed it was possible to establish their program for society by democratic means and without overthrowing the state. Liebknecht's son, Karl, was also active in the Social Democratic party, and in 1919, after release from prison for antiwar activities, he founded the revolutionary Spartacist League. The Spartacists later became the German Communist party (the KPD).

Ludwig Frahm wholeheartedly embraced the ideas and promises of social democracy. For him, they represented nothing less than salvation for society. His political enthusiasm for the Social Democratic party and its principles was passed easily to his impressionable young grandson.

Once in school, Herbert quickly established himself as an outstanding student. In recognition of his achievements, he was pushed ahead from the lower-level *Volksschule* to Lübeck's *Realschule* — the equivalent of an American high school — when he was 13. The following year, he was awarded a scholarship to enter the Johanneum, a prestigious private school otherwise inaccessible to a student whose family was not well off.

Herbert looked forward to going to school each day. German language and history were his favorite subjects. Both were taught by Eilhard Erich Pauls, who quickly noticed Herbert's enthusiasm for reading and writing. A kindly schoolmaster, Pauls encouraged the boy, demanding excellence from him in the classroom but not interfering with Herbert's growing fascination with politics.

Against the advice of others on the Johanneum staff, Pauls gave Herbert permission to write a final paper on the controversial socialist leader August Bebel. Bebel, a friend and close associate of Wilhelm Liebknecht, was immensely popular in Mecklenburg. In 1901 it was Bebel who declared the city of Lübeck "a citadel of Social Democracy." However, another of Herbert's professors was not so favorably impressed with either the boy's politics or his writings. The professor called Herbert's mother in for a discussion. He warned Martha Frahm to keep her son away from politics. She was told that Herbert was a gifted boy but that politics would only ruin him.

But Herbert would not be swayed. With Pauls's continued support, the boy took the first tentative steps of what would become his journalistic and political career and submitted articles to Lübeck's Social Democratic newspaper, *Volksbote*. This newspaper was read dutifully by the city's 30,000 workers. The first article that Herbert published earned him five *Reichsmark*; another won him a prize. Success built his confidence and brought him to the attention of Julius Leber, the editor of *Volksbote*. Leber was also a popular Social Democratic politician. He was impressed with Frahm's writing.

By 1929, Frahm was leading the Karl Marx Group of the Socialist Worker Youth in Lübeck, and boldly wearing the organization's uniform at the Johanneum. Leber admired the teenager's political ideas and the courage with which he expressed them. Before long, he took an active interest in Frahm's work and education, quickly becoming his journalistic and political mentor.

The socialist August Bebel helped found the Social Democratic party in 1875. The Social Democrats were Germany's largest party by 1912 and were less extreme than the German Communist party (KPD).

3

Mentor and Opponent

By 1930 Herbert Frahm's boyhood was over. At the age of 17 he had grown to be a young man of above-average height with thick, wavy brown hair, a lock of which seemed to hang perpetually over his forehead. The young women he met at the Social Democratic youth activities found him very attractive. While still a teenager, Frahm was an active journalist, writing about Germany's embittered and restless young people. Leber himself wrote about the growing danger that many young Germans might fall prey to Hitler's violent nationalism. At this time Frahm was living, as many working-class youths did, within the social framework set up by the Social Democratic party. The party provided an entire galaxy of activities for young people, which included sports, socials, and community service.

Like many young men his age, Frahm tried to camouflage his adolescence by adopting what seemed to him to be the more adult habits of his fellow journalists. Soon he was smoking cigarettes and drinking in the beer halls, talking with other journalists and with workers.

His activity and example had a strong impact on my thinking and on my work. He exercised a lasting influence on my whole life. I had grown up without a father. There was an emptiness in my life. Leber filled it.
—WILLY BRANDT
on Julius Leber

Willy Brandt in 1932. After the Socialist Worker Youth was disbanded by the Social Democrats' leadership for being too radical, Brandt supported leftist Reichstag representatives Max Seydewitz and Kurt Rosenfeld, who founded the Socialist Workers party (SAP) in 1931.

Julius Leber was arrested in 1933 and spent most of the next decade in jail during the Nazi regime. Although Brandt challenged Leber and other mainstream Social Democrats, he continued Leber's struggle against the Nazis, devoting himself to the underground that opposed Adolf Hitler.

By now Frahm's opinions were no longer shaped at home. Ludwig Frahm's once pervasive authority over his grandson gave way to the professional influence and direction of Pauls and Julius Leber. Nevertheless the young man's first steps into the political arena had been deeply influenced by the convictions of his grandfather. Perhaps it was his grandfather's storytelling about the past that served to encourage Frahm to write articles about the explosive events then taking place around him.

Leber proved to have an electrifying effect on Frahm. They had so much in common that their becoming mentor and protégé was practically inevitable. Both came from the working class and, through hard work and academic achievement, both pushed beyond the barriers that tended to accompany their economic station.

In Leber, Frahm saw a man whose views reflected his own — the belief that democracy was a system of government that could end injustice and poverty. Frahm's own enthusiasm for these ideals was a revelation to Leber, who had once written that "the younger generation with their great feelings of unsatisfied disappointment . . . are a breeding ground for enemies of the state." Herbert Frahm seemed the exception, and for a while he gave Leber hope for the next generation of Social Democrats.

On May 6, 1930, *Volksbote* published an article by "H. F." that ran under the headline "We and the Parental Home."

"Our parents shouldn't say now: 'We weren't allowed to do that at your age'," H. F. wrote. "No, they should allow young people more liberty. For we need strength and freedom, friendship and trust, if we want to win a world, dear older comrades, along our own path."

The article provoked an uneasiness among older readers, and brought disapproval from the Social Democratic establishment, who regarded the young writer as too impatient and arrogant. At the same time, it was welcomed enthusiastically by Lübeck's younger generation. [With the local notoriety that suddenly surrounded the anonymous H. F., "Willy

Brandt" came into being.] Frahm began using "Willy Brandt" as his pen name and as his identification within the Social Democratic party.

Leber did not ignore the controversy surrounding his protégé when he helped Frahm obtain official membership in the Social Democratic party. Although he had not yet reached the mandatory minimum age of 18, young Frahm's popularity had already created for him a modest following in the Social Democratic youth movement.

A faction within the Social Democrats' leadership disapproved of Frahm's notoriety as Willy Brandt and attempted to block his acceptance into the party. But Leber used his own substantial influence to dispel any serious doubts about Frahm's sincere commitment to social democracy. Consequently, before Herbert Frahm celebrated his 18th birthday, Willy Brandt was registered as a full member of the Social Democratic party.

It was not long before Willy Brandt found himself again at the center of controversy. By the spring of 1930, the differences between the younger, more liberal members and the older, more conservative and established Social Democrats had developed into a serious conflict.

Hitler stands with fellow participants in the Beer Hall *Putsch* (uprising) of 1923. They attempted to overthrow the Weimar republic, which had been created primarily under Social Democratic leadership. Ernst Röhm (second from right) came to lead the storm troopers. General Erich von Ludendorff (center) was a key German strategist in World War I.

Citizens form a soup line in Berlin (circa 1930) during the Great Depression. Hitler gained supporters during the economic hardship in Germany that followed the New York Stock Exchange crash. Meanwhile, Brandt observed the Social Democrats' increasing confusion.

In 1931 two Reichstag representatives, Max Seydewitz and Kurt Rosenfeld, broke away from the Social Democratic mainstream and created the more radical Socialist Workers party, the SAP. The Socialist Youth Organization, (*Jungsozialisten*), joined this new party almost at once. Frahm was among those who joined. During this time, Frahm read an editorial in a rival publication comparing the prominent Social Democrat Karl Liebknecht, who was murdered by government troops in 1919, to Hitler. Hitler had joined the right-wing German Workers party in 1919 and from it created the Nazi party. In a decade's time, Hitler made his hatred for the Social Democrats well known throughout Germany.

Frahm was incensed by the article, which, he thought, was an insult to both Liebknecht and the socialists. He immediately wrote a letter to the journal, criticizing the editor — a Social Democrat himself — and asking how he could allow the Nazis to see Social Democrats viciously attacking one another. When Frahm's letter appeared in the following issue, he received an official reprimand from the Social Democratic party.

Leber could not always run interference for Frahm's impulsive alter ego, Willy Brandt. After being chastised for attacking the editorial, Frahm was taken aside by Leber, who advised him to be more cautious and not so quick off the mark. Leber suggested that he not send off his letters in the heat of the moment, but to wait until the next day, and then edit his own work. That way he could be more cool-headed and less prone to giving offense. Frahm wisely heeded Leber's suggestions about avoiding unnecessary political disputes. The next article published in *Volksbote* by Willy Brandt was about "the social significance" of fishing.

But all was not well for Germany and its majority political party, the SPD. Few Germans felt as confident as young Willy Brandt. For most, day-to-day existence was a struggle against escalating economic hardship. Economic disruption caused by World War I and the enormous reparations owed to the Allies under the Treaty of Versailles led to sky-rocketing inflation by 1923. German money had become virtually worthless. With help from the United States, the German economy began to improve during the mid-1920s, but the Great Depression that struck in the United States in 1929 wiped out the short-lived stability. By 1931 more than 5 million Germans were unemployed. In July of that year, Germany's three most important banks were closed.

Club-wielding storm troopers burst in on a meeting of German communists and mayhem ensues. The Nazis frequently battled both the communists and the Social Democrats in the streets. Brandt himself was rumored to have taken part in one such confrontation.

Riots erupted across Germany as old passions and fears were inflamed by the increasingly desperate conditions. The Weimar government, established under primarily Social Democratic leadership after the war, was nearly paralyzed, slowly crumbling under the strain of the political conflict within its own ranks. At the same time, extremist political organizations — Hitler's growing Nazi party on the Right and the German Communist party on the Left — attacked the Social Democrats, who still held a majority in the Reichstag.

As early as 1929, many Social Democrats, including Julius Leber, were near despair, and felt that a strong military buildup should be implemented if the Social Democrats were to gain the political control necessary to solve the almost overwhelming economic depression. A military build up would, they hoped, restore some degree of pride in the defeated nation, and also stimulate the economy. They felt that this could be accomplished by putting new armored vehicles into production.

For the first time, Brandt openly disagreed with Leber. He and other young socialists viewed such a proposal as ridiculous — an outright violation of the provisions of the Treaty of Versailles that risked in-

Leber (third from left) confers with other leading Social Democrats during the Great Depression. Disagreeing with Brandt on the issue of rearmament, Leber thought that building armored military vehicles was worthwhile if it helped to strengthen both the economy and democracy.

curring the Allied forces' wrath. They also believed it was more important, at that moment, to concentrate their efforts on providing food for the hungry and jobs for the unemployed. As the best known member of the SAP faction, Brandt became their spokesperson. Soon, at party meetings, he was publicly challenging Leber and the established Social Democrats.

Brandt and a group of young leftist Social Democrats from the rank-and-file membership tried to attend one such meeting at which Leber was scheduled to speak. Although initially denied entrance, they were finally admitted at Leber's suggestion, in order to avoid another display of disunity within the party.

After Leber's speech, Brandt asked to be heard. Brandt spontaneously addressed a crowd numbering more than 2,000. Despite attempts to shout him down Brandt stood firm, defiantly pounding his fist on the podium.

"What do these kids know?" a senior official shouted, rising from his seat in the auditorium. Brandt stopped speaking, stared directly at the official confronting him, and replied that although he was young, he still knew something about what was happening.

That evening tempers grew hotter and ultimately punches were thrown as one faction attempted to outshout and discredit the other. Leber made an effort to speak to Brandt in the midst of the mayhem but was whisked off stage before Brandt could hear him. The fighting among Social Democrats that spilled out into the streets of Lübeck that night served only to further weaken moderate forces in the national government in Berlin. For the next two years, the Social Democrats were unable to agree upon one course of action. Moderates in the Weimar government, their ideas and energy exhausted, found it increasingly harder to protect the republic from disaster. Previously, such disorganization would have been merely a political setback. But now the Social Democrats faced disaster; Germany was ripe for a dynamic and charismatic leader of any political stripe to seize control.

The Steel Helmet, an organization for German veterans of World War I, holds a rally. Its members included famed field marshal and president of the Weimar republic Paul von Hindenburg.

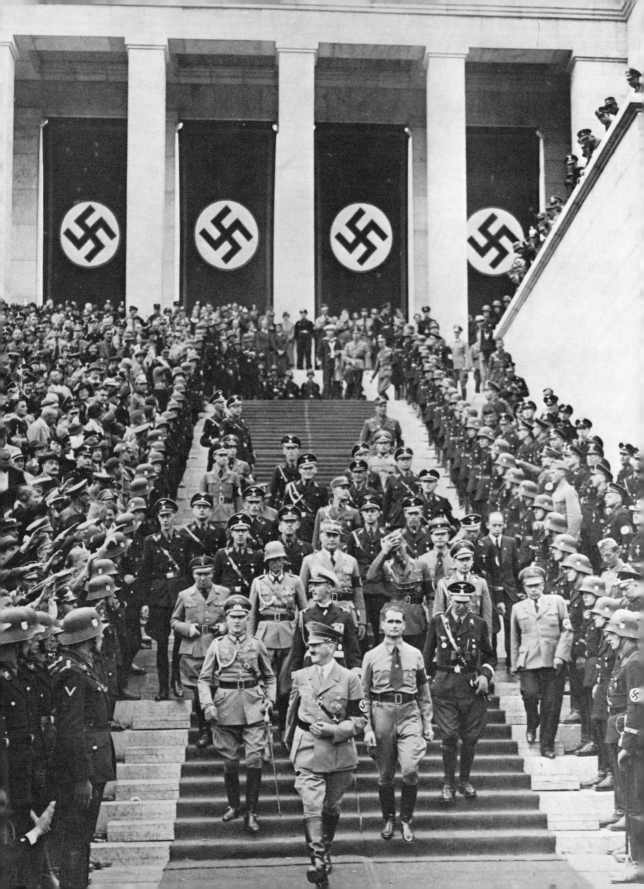

4
Descent into Terror

The Reichstag elections of September 14, 1930, marked the first significant change in German politics since the Weimar Constitution was established in 1919 after World War I. Hitler's Nazi party was emboldened by the political blunders and shortcomings of the Social Democrats. But that year even the Nazis were surprised when they abruptly found themselves the second most powerful political party in the land, winning 107 seats. The German Communist party also increased its strength to 77 seats. Both parties' gains were at the expense of the Social Democrats, who still managed to maintain the largest number of seats but were now unable to put together a sufficient majority to pass any legislation on their own.

Once dismissed merely as another lunatic extremist on the fringes of national politics, Hitler suddenly captured the attention of the German people. Hitler was a gifted public speaker. His spellbinding oratory, laden with nationalistic symbolism and emotional showmanship, electrified a growing segment of the public.

Rather an end with horror than horrors without end.
—Nazi slogan prior to 1930 elections

Dictator Adolf Hitler and high-ranking Nazi officials, including Rudolf Hess (front, right), attend one of the mass rallies the Nazis held in Nuremberg. During the mid-1930s the Nazis consolidated power. To establish opposition to Hitler outside Germany, Brandt went into exile in 1933.

Hitler, Hess, and fellow Nazis prepare to meet with representatives of other German nationalist parties in Bad Harzburg in 1931. Despite a drop in the Nazis' popularity in the Reichstag elections in November 1932, the Social Democrats failed to reverse the Nazis' huge gains. Brandt, with other members of the SAP, went to Denmark and Norway.

"We shall banish want. We shall banish fear. The essence of National Socialism is human welfare," Hitler promised, speaking at a Nazi rally in Berlin just before the 1930 elections. "National Socialism is the revolution of the common man!" he proclaimed. To a people weary of unrest and hardship, Hitler's stirring promises were a welcome and exciting relief. His speeches began to bristle with race hatred and his own doctrine of German racial supremacy. The Germans, he asserted, were actually a super race called Aryans. "The Aryan race has a right to rule the world," he shouted at an outdoor rally in Nuremberg. "We must make this right the guiding star of foreign policy . . . It will not be the neutrals or lukewarms who make history!"

To his opponents' bewilderment, the more aggressive his speeches became, the more people came under his spell. Hitler appealed to those who felt deeply wronged by events since the war: the millions of unemployed, veterans embittered by defeat, businessmen who had lost everything in the economic collapse. Someone, they thought, must be to blame; Hitler provided scapegoats, objects for their rage. The Nazis took their message into the streets, handing out leaflets and beating anyone who refused to take them.

Already Nazi storm troopers, led by Ernst Röhm, had grown in number to 100,000. They eventually became so numerous that Hitler feared they might become a threat to his own control of the Nazi party. Many in its top leadership wanted to take over traditional institutions such as the German army's officer corps and topple big business. Hitler needed the loyalty of both business and the army. The Nazi military elite called the SS, *Schützstaffeln* (armed guard), had also been established as part of the SA. This organization was created to serve as Hitler's personal bodyguard and to enforce his will within the Nazi party. In June 1934 key leaders of the SA, including Röhm, were seized on Hitler's orders and executed in the Night of the Long Knives.

Despite their disagreements over the direction of Social Democratic policy, both Leber and Brandt were shaken by Hitler's startling political gains. In a rare display of party unity, the Social Democrats organized a massive public meeting in Lübeck — still a Social Democratic stronghold — in order to display their opposition to Hitler and the Nazis. Leber and Brandt were allies united in a common cause, but events were moving beyond the control of both men.

The German Communist party celebrates May Day in Berlin in 1932. Confident that the Nazis were only a symptom of the capitalist system's downfall, the Communists helped the Nazis undermine the Social Democrats. Brandt was shocked by his countrymen's increasing support for Hitler.

Hitler greets the Weimar republic's last president, Paul von Hindenburg, in March 1933, following Hitler's appointment as chancellor. In Lübeck Brandt saw that Hitler would brutally suppress Social Democratic leaders such as Leber, who spoke in defense of freedom.

Hitler considered Leber to be a dangerous opponent — perhaps the only one who might stir the masses into action against his rising Nazi regime. Leber's popularity — even with Social Democrats such as Brandt who did not entirely share his views — made him too prominent to be ignored. Hitler decided the protest rally would be the ideal opportunity to send a message of his own to the city of Lübeck, Leber, and the Social Democratic opposition. Thousands gathered in Lübeck for the mass meeting. Those who could not get into the city's public auditorium gathered outside in the streets. Leber spoke at the rally.

"We are in the midst of a counterrevolution," he said. "But we declare: Our movement is strong. History is on the side of freedom, and freedom will be with you as long as you fight for it. . . . Victory or no victory, if one fights for liberty one doesn't ask what tomorrow will bring."

The crowd rose cheering, fists clenched in the sign of workers' solidarity. Suddenly a commotion outside in the street was heard above the applause. A moment later storm troopers burst into the hall and began bludgeoning their way toward the podium.

"Leber stood alone on stage," Brandt stated years later, recalling the fighting that broke out that night. "The Nazis thought they could finish him. But they were wrong. Leber smashed a chair, took a chair leg in one hand and . . . clubbed his way through the murder-thirsty mob to safety."

Circumstances became more bleak for the Social Democrats. The Nazis eventually overtook them as the largest party in the Reichstag. Early that same year, those members of the German Communist party who were not sufficiently radical were expelled from the party. Nevertheless, these former KPD members were too radical for the Social Democrats, and many joined the SAP. By now Frahm had fin-

A storm trooper accompanies a policeman with a muzzled dog in Berlin. Soon after Hitler's rise to power, the police began to actively enforce Nazi policies. On one occasion, Leber fought off Nazi attackers with a chair leg.

In May 1933 storm troopers participate in a favorite Nazi tactic against ideas they considered dangerous: book burning. The Nazis destroyed works that did not fit into their creed of German nationalism and racial supremacy. German novelist Thomas Mann called Nazism "a revolution . . . opposed to ideas, to everything higher. . . ."

ished his education at the Johanneum and was an apprentice with a shipping company. For the moment it seemed Hitler's appeal was on the wane. Although their chances to stop the Nazis were fading, the Social Democrats and the Communists did not combine political forces against them in the elections of November 1932, when the Nazis actually experienced a slight decline in popularity. It was the last chance either party would have to peacefully prevent the Nazis from gaining power. Early in the new year, an elderly and enfeebled President Hindenburg was convinced by conservative advisers to appoint Adolf Hitler as chancellor. When Hitler came to power the SAP was officially disbanded by Seydewitz and Rosenfeld, but underground splinter groups persisted.

Violence erupted across Germany as storm troopers, the SS, and the Gestapo competed to crush any opponents in an effort to win Hitler's approval and secure their own position within the Nazi *Reich*, or empire.

Physicist Albert Einstein, at home in Berlin in the 1920s. Einstein and Austrian psychoanalyst Sigmund Freud, both Jewish, narrowly escaped Hitler's policies of racial terror and genocide.

Those, such as Brandt, who managed to escape this first wave of terror, understood that any German courageous enough to defy the Nazis' iron fist would have to operate in secret, as part of an underground. Brandt recalls that the SAP's members believed that their organization "constituted the core of the 'new' party of the German Left."

That night, before leaving Lübeck, Brandt saw a former editor for *Volksbote* being shoved and kicked through the streets by an angry mob. Hanging around the terrified man's neck was a sign that read "Jewish pig."

The sight sickened and infuriated Brandt. During the coming years, such Nazi persecution of Jews would become commonplace in Germany. Concentration camps, slave labor, and genocide would soon become Hitler's policy toward Europe's Jews, communists, "non-Aryans," and any individual or group who resisted the Nazis. Yet there was nothing he could do that would not jeopardize himself and the important task he would undertake the next day. As the mob disappeared into the darkness, Brandt resolved that although he had been powerless to help his friend this time, making good his escape would enable him and others like him to destroy Hitler's terrible hold on Germany.

Questions, one after another, filled his head as he stood silently in the darkened doorway. How could his own people become the enemy? Why were so many unable to see beyond Hitler's bombast and promises? The sound of a brick tossed through a nearby grocer's window startled Brandt. He must move on. There was not a minute to spare.

Hitler and Röhm, leader of the storm troopers, pay tribute to Germany's Unknown Soldier at Nuremberg in 1933. Such vast spectacles enabled Hitler to intensify his already hypnotic hold on the German masses.

Late that night, Brandt said goodbye to his mother and grandfather. Ludwig Frahm sat across the room in a large, overstuffed chair. He seemed feeble now, hardly the robust storyteller of Brandt's childhood. The old man had never forgiven his grandson for questioning the wisdom of Leber and the Social Democratic establishment. But as Willy wrapped his arms around his grandfather in a hug, the old man gently patted his back, silently wishing him well.

Brandt disappeared from Lübeck. Those who thought they saw him were assured by others that they were mistaken. Brandt had slipped away through the icy Baltic waters into exile in Denmark, leaving only rumors in his wake. From Denmark, 20-year-old Brandt would make his way to temporary safety in Oslo, Norway's capital city.

As members of the SS, or *Schützstaffeln*, look on, small children salute the *Führer* (leader) in 1937. Under Hitler, the education of German children was completely controlled by the Nazi state.

5

Adventure and Exile

In 1933, Copenhagen, the Danish capital, suddenly became a haven for German political exiles. The Nazi takeover in Germany was powerfully felt in Denmark. But as ominous as the refugees' stories were, few outside Germany could fully understand Hitler's ruthlessness, or the dark days that lay ahead.

"My Danish friends intimated they thought the stories about the cruelties in Germany were very much exaggerated," Brandt wrote years later. "Were too pessimistic when we declared Hitler plunge the world into war?"

After several days in Copenhagen, where Brandt stayed briefly with a leftist poet named Oscar Hansen, he boarded a boat for Oslo, Norway. There he was to meet Finn Moe, editor of *Arbeiderbladet*, the newspaper of the Norwegian Labor party *Det Norske Arbeiderparti*, or DNA. Moe had been a correspondent in Berlin from 1927 to 1932. He was ready to assist any German political exile with ties to the Social Democrats. With Moe's help, Brandt, who quickly learned the Norwegian language, was appointed head of the Norwegian Refugee Federation.

You don't know it, the heart-asthma of the exile, the uprooting, the nervous terror of homelessness.
—THOMAS MANN
German novelist

Oslo, capital city of Norway, during the 1930s. After an attempt to place a member of the underground outside Germany ended in arrest, Brandt was chosen by fellow socialists to go first to Denmark, where he stayed with the Danish poet Oscar Hansen, and then to Norway.

In June 1933 the Nazis banned the Social Democratic party. Nazi secret police were also on the SAP's trail in Germany. The organization's activities were under direct attack. During the spring of 1933, 91 SAP members were arrested in Dresden; that summer, members of the SAP in Breslau were brutally tortured by the Nazis. In Berlin the SAP was destroyed. During this period, a young woman named Gertrud Meyer obtained a passport and left her parents' home in Lübeck. She was a member of the underground, and she was bound for Oslo to join Brandt there. She had been Brandt's girlfriend since the time he had become a journalist at the age of 16. When it became certain that Brandt would be leaving for Norway, Gertrud had pleaded to be allowed to accompany him but had been forbidden to leave Lübeck at the same time for fear her movements would arouse suspicion. With Brandt safely based in Norway, she went into exile. Together, "Trudel," as she was called, and Willy set up housekeeping in Oslo. She was extremely courageous and once, while held by the Nazis, swallowed a letter from Brandt and revealed nothing to her interrogators. Although they had not married, Brandt introduced Gertrud as his wife to their new acquaintances. Brandt's first year in exile transpired without incident. He tried desperately to remain in contact with the small number of SPD members who were not yet jailed or killed in Germany. As the Nazis hunted down his comrades, Brandt continued to play an important role in the Norwegian-based German resistance.

In 1934 a campaign began among Germans abroad to nominate Carl von Ossietzky, a noted German writer, for the Nobel Peace Prize. Ossietzky — a pacifist — had been imprisoned by the Nazis. A courageous man, Ossietzky had continued to denounce Hitler's tactics of deceit and violence. Brandt and others hoped the campaign for Ossietzky would focus world attention on the Nazis' trampling of all human rights. Furious with the Ossietzky movement, Hitler cabled a warning to the Norwegian government not to offend Germany by honoring "a state criminal."

With friends and contacts, Brandt lobbied strenuously for the Norwegian government not to give in to Hitler's threat, but in 1935 no prize was awarded. (The final decision concerning the Nobel Prize is made every year by a committee of the Norwegian parliament, or *Storting*). On November 26 of the following year, however, the Nobel committee awarded Ossietzky the Nobel Peace Prize for 1936.

Not surprisingly, Ossietzky was refused the Nazis' permission to travel to Oslo for his award. In response to the Nobel committee's defiance, Hitler prohibited any citizen of the Third Reich, as Hitler's government was called, from accepting the prize in the future.

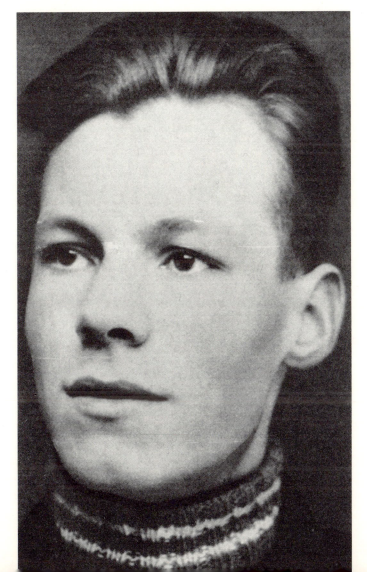

Brandt in exile in Norway, 1934. Within a year after his arrival, he began writing for Scandinavian socialist newspapers and befriended Norwegian socialists. By 1938 Brandt's German citizenship under the name Herbert Frahm had been revoked by the Nazis, and he became a hunted man.

German writer Carl von Ossietzky won the Nobel Peace Prize in 1936 but was unable to receive the award because he was imprisoned by the Nazis. Working closely with the Nobel Foundation and with the Norwegian government, Brandt championed Ossietzky as a deserving recipient of the prize.

In June 1936 Brandt received orders from the underground to return to Berlin, but it was virtually impossible for him to reenter Germany as either Willy Brandt or Herbert Frahm. Gertrud Meyer provided a solution to this problem. Continuing to live with Brandt, she married a member of the Norwegian Youth Federation, Gunnar Gaasland, in order to obtain the political security of Norwegian citizenship. Gaasland was friendly with both Meyer and Brandt. Realizing the danger his German friends faced, he decided to take part in the scheme. When Gaasland, a native-born Norwegian, was issued a passport, Meyer persuaded him to hand it over to Brandt. Another friend substituted Brandt's photograph for Gaasland's while Brandt practiced signing Gaasland's signature. For the next three years, the passport never failed him.

When Brandt arrived in Berlin, the Gestapo was everywhere. Disguised as a foreign student, Brandt gathered information for the underground. He had to avoid old acquaintances, who might now be loyal Nazis. Meanwhile, tensions between the SAP and the communists in Germany were escalating, with the communists actually calling the SAP a front for the Gestapo.

Before leaving Germany Brandt arranged to visit his mother, who told him that his grandfather had committed suicide. The dashed dreams of his beloved Social Democratic party, coupled with his grandson's exile, had overwhelmed the proud old man. His death left his grandson bitter and heartbroken.

"I felt much older," Brandt later wrote. "My Lübeck childhood was far, far away and I was depressed by the knowledge that my mother had to endure interrogations . . . on account of me. But Mother had not a single word of reproach."

On returning to Oslo, Brandt continued to work with the Norwegian Youth Federation and to help the hundreds of German refugees still flowing into the city. Nevertheless, he became restless and wanted to travel.

Though Nazis had clashed with communists in street fighting prior to Hitler's rise to power, the conflict ended decisively in Nazi victory when Hitler was appointed chancellor. In Spain, however, a similar conflict exploded into civil war between militant nationalists and the forces of the Spanish republic. Brandt saw this war as significant for Europe and he wanted to observe the conflict firsthand. Gertrud was not happy with his plans but knew she could not prevent Brandt from leaving Oslo. He traveled as Gunnar Gaasland and sent articles back to Oslo for publication.

Brandt was not alone; Germany's Nazi government and Italy's Fascist dictatorship headed by Benito Mussolini were also very interested in Spain. There, they could both help bring another right-wing dictator — Francisco Franco — to power, and simultaneously test new weapons and military equipment. Republican forces received help from the Soviet Union. (The war ended with Franco's victory in 1939.) While in Spain, Brandt stayed at the headquarters of the United Marxist Workers party, or POUM (Partido Obrero de Unificación Marxista). The POUM was an independent Marxist organization that was hostile to Spanish communists but joined with them in a coalition called the Popular

Brandt traveled to Spain as a correspondent during the Spanish Civil War (1936–39). He stayed in Barcelona at the headquarters of the POUM (United Marxist Workers' party), which fought to defend the Spanish republic against the nationalist general Francisco Franco.

Front to defend the Spanish republic. From Spain, Brandt went on to Paris to report on the activities of French socialists.

In September 1938, while in Paris, Brandt learned that his German citizenship had been revoked. The Gestapo now considered Herbert Frahm an "enemy of the Reich" and a warrant was issued for his arrest. Brandt returned to Oslo and upon the advice of Finn Moe began using a second pseudonym, F. Franke, as his by-line.

Brandt's relationship with Gertrud Meyer did not withstand their stressful lives in the underground. Meyer left Oslo for the United States. Brandt then promptly renewed his friendship with Carlota Thorkildsen whom he had first met while working with the Nobel Foundation during the Ossietzky campaign. Thorkildsen was nine years older than Brandt. To the young man from the working-class city of Lübeck, the more intellectual Carlota possessed an air of sophistication and elegance.

In March 1938 Hitler absorbed nearby Austria into the Reich, an action known historically as the *Anschluss*. Later that year, the Nazis seized the Sudetenland in Czechoslovakia after Hitler persuaded British prime minister Neville Chamberlain that he would make no more territorial claims. Germany invaded Poland on September 1, 1939, in a spectacular demonstration of a new type of warfare called *blitzkrieg*, or lightning attack, in which fighter-bombers supported a fast-moving onslaught of tanks and troops.

Two days later, on September 3, after unsuccessful efforts to obtain a German withdrawal from Polish territory, Britain and France declared war. On September 17, in accordance with the Nazi-Soviet nonaggression pact signed in August, the Soviet Union attacked Poland from the east. (This pact did not last long, for the Germans subsequently invaded the Soviet Union in June 1941.) Ten days later, Poland surrendered. Just as Brandt and other Germans in the resistance anticipated, Hitler had made another world war inevitable.

In Berlin, a city now festooned with swastika ban-

ners, few wished to remember Hitler's speech nearly six years earlier on November 10, 1933: "I am not so senseless as to want war," Hitler had told the world. "We want peace and understanding, nothing else. We want to give our hand to our former enemies. When has Germany ever broken its word?" For Norway and German exile Willy Brandt, it was only a matter of time before promises already broken led to disastrous consequences.

Brandt and Carlota returned from a brief vacation in the mountains outside Oslo in the spring of 1940. On April 8, news filtered into the city that the Nazis would soon launch an invasion of Norway. That same day, Carlota learned that she was pregnant. The following day Brandt and Thorkildsen were awakened by the telephone. On the other end, a friend's voice exclaimed that German warships had entered the Oslo Fjord, one of Norway's many coastal inlets with high cliffs on either side. German troops were less than 24 hours away.

Brandt was in very grave danger. He had been on the Gestapo's death list for at least two years. With the Germans in Norway, Brandt had to leave the country at once. Thorkildsen would stay behind with friends and join him later.

German foreign minister Joachim von Ribbentrop (right) and his Soviet counterpart sign the German-Soviet nonaggression pact on December 14, 1939. The agreement enabled Hitler to concentrate on western conquests, such as that of Norway in 1940.

King Haakon VII of Norway with Prime Minister Johann Nygaardsvold (right) in London, 1941. Haakon, who had refused to recognize Hitler's threats, established a Norwegian government in exile after the German invasion. Brandt escaped to neutral Sweden.

In the meantime, Norwegian king Haakon VII received a message from Hitler's envoy. Knowing that German bomber aircraft and seaborne troops were ready to attack, Haakon slowly opened and read the cable. It was an ultimatum. The Norwegian government must instantly accept "the protection of the Reich," the letter explained. If Norway refused, "any resistance would be broken by all possible means."

Haakon refused. He also refused to appoint as Norway's premier the Nazi collaborator Vidkun Quisling, whose name later became synonymous with Nazi-inspired acts of treason against the Allies. But Hitler's promised invasion was delayed for a day by heavy damage inflicted on the two main German transport ships by a handful of heroic Norwegian sailors. This delay allowed Haakon to flee to London with 20 truckloads of Norway's gold reserves, where he and his cabinet established a government in exile.

Brandt's escape was not so auspicious. After driving with a group of Norwegian socialists to within 160 miles of the Swedish border, their car was stopped by officials already loyal to the Nazis. Once again, Brandt's forged passport identifying him as Gunnar Gaasland saved the day. Although the officials were under orders from the Nazis to detain any German exiles attempting to leave the country, they allowed what they thought were the automobile's Norwegian passengers to depart on foot. Brandt narrowly escaped detection, but to reach Sweden, he and his friends would have to cross more than 100 miles of snow-covered Norwegian terrain.

It seemed hopeless until, not far from the roadblock, Brandt and his friends encountered a unit of Norwegian soldiers. Brandt recognized two of them as friends from Oslo. They advised him to put on a Norwegian army uniform and accompany their unit. Two days later the unit was intercepted by German soldiers and ordered to surrender. Brandt passed the next four weeks as an unlucky Norwegian soldier in a prisoner-of-war camp. In June Brandt was given a railroad pass and told to return to his "hometown" of Oslo. After a brief reunion with

Hitler's Europe in 1942

Legend:
- Hitler's Germany
- Territory conquered by Axis Powers
- Germany's Axis Allies
- Nations cooperating with Nazis
- Nazi-occupied, self administered region
- Neutral

Nine years after Hitler became chancellor, and replaced the Weimar republic with a one-party dictatorship, German armies had overrun most of Europe. By 1942, Hitler had conquered more territory than had the 18th-century French military leader and emperor Napoleon Bonaparte.

Vidkun Quisling, former Norwegian defense minister, inspects German troops as head of the puppet government the Nazis installed in Norway in 1940. The label "Quisling" was applied to anyone who betrayed his homeland or the Allies during the war with Hitler.

Carlota, Brandt determined that it was still unwise to remain in Norway.

In July Brandt again set out by car, getting to within five miles of the Swedish border. There, with the help of a guide, he hiked across the frontier, successfully avoiding the German patrols. At twilight he crossed into neutral Sweden and declared himself a political fugitive from Germany. With the help of friends he had met in Barcelona during the Spanish Civil War, Swedish authorities granted Brandt's release from interrogation.

In Stockholm, the Swedish capital, Brandt received Norwegian citizenship from Haakon's government in exile. He also received the welcome news of the birth of his daughter, Ninja. Through connections in Oslo, Brandt arranged for Carlota and the baby to join him in Stockholm. He and Carlota were married soon after she arrived.

By 1941 Willy Brandt had been in exile for eight years. The German resistance was crumbling. Those members who still managed to survive operated in small, independent groups. Although the underground fought with determination and bravery, they were no match for Hitler's ruthless Gestapo.

For the next three years Brandt continued his journalistic activities, publishing articles and two books, *War in Norway* and *Norway Fights On*. In 1942 he wrote a ground-breaking book on changes in warfare, entitled *Guerillakriget* (*Guerrilla War*). By 1944, however, Brandt's attention was drawn back to the German resistance. Once again, it was Julius Leber who appeared at the center of the struggle.

Julius Leber was put on trial for his part in a right-wing conspiracy, called the Kreisau Circle, to overthrow Hitler. Brandt's mentor was seized by the *Gestapo*, the Nazi secret police, in 1944, and was executed for his part in the plot.

Soldiers of the Soviet Red Army raise their nation's flag in Berlin in 1945. The German armies, which invaded the Soviet Union in 1941, made a final defensive stand in May 1945 against the Soviets, whose counterattack swept into Germany.

After 11 years in prison, Leber was released. With most of his old Social Democratic comrades dead or exiled, Leber, thought Hitler, must by now be a broken man. Hitler was mistaken. Within months of his release, Leber contacted a group of right-wing nationalists worried that Hitler preferred to destroy Germany than admit defeat. A plot was initiated to eliminate Hitler.

Brandt, meanwhile, was overjoyed to learn of Leber's release, as well as his involvement in this highly dangerous conspiracy. Brandt was later cautiously approached by these anti-Nazis about his own interest in forming a new German government that would replace Hitler and unconditionally end the war. Brandt's response, of course, was affirmative. But before plans could be implemented, Leber and most of his coconspirators were betrayed and arrested. A desperate and unsuccessful attempt on Hitler's life by the few remaining right-wing conspirators led to dire consequences. None survived Hitler's vengeance.

When Brandt heard of these events and Leber's execution, he wept. Julius Leber had seemed almost indestructible. All hope was gone for Hitler's removal by a German-initiated coup. But the tide of the war had turned against Hitler. Germany was about to collapse, fighting British and United States forces in western Europe and North Africa, while losing battle after battle to Soviet forces in the east. When Soviet-led army troops overran the bomb-shattered city of Berlin in April 1945, Hitler committed suicide in his bunker with Eva Braun, his mistress. Their bodies were burned outside the devastated Berlin Reich Chancellery. On May 2 the Soviets captured the city. Hitler's Reich had been finally destroyed.

On May 8, 1945, Germany surrendered unconditionally to the Allied military commanders in Rheims, France. The German commander in chief in Norway, General Franz Böhme, signed an order surrendering his 310,000 troops. In the closing days of the war Brandt made a telephone call to Nazi SS headquarters in Norway to confirm rumors that Norwegian political prisoners — many of whom he knew — had been released. He spoke directly with an SS officer, who would commit suicide only days later. Brandt remained in Stockholm for two days. In Oslo the newly liberated Norwegians celebrated the Allied victory. Although he was glad that the Nazi war machine had at last been halted, he could not completely share in the victors' joy over Germany's defeat, which left Germany divided and in ruins. Brandt's 12-year exile from his homeland was over. On May 10 Brandt left Stockholm and arrived with Carlota and Ninja in Oslo. He remained a Norwegian citizen for the next three years.

His marriage to Carlota Thorkildsen had not survived what he called "external circumstances." The couple had separated in 1944. That same year, Brandt had begun an affair with Rut Hansen, who for a time had worked as his and Carlota's maid in Stockholm. When he returned to Germany in 1947, Rut followed and set up housekeeping. By the following year, he and Carlota were officially divorced.

> *Nazism is not completely overcome. As a regime it is destroyed. As a spiritual pestilence we still find it or a mentality related to it in the heads of many people, I am sorry to say.*
> —WILLY BRANDT
> on returning to Germany

6

A City Divided

Germany in the spring of 1945 had been rendered helpless by the Nazi dictatorship's defeat. Japan's bid to control Asia and the Pacific islands came to a halt in August, shortly after the cities of Hiroshima and Nagasaki were destroyed by atomic bombs dropped by the United States. Italy, the third partner in the alliance with Hitler's Germany, known as the Axis powers, surrendered.

The victorious Allies, under the provisions of the Yalta Agreement, signed in February by U.S. president Franklin Roosevelt, Great Britain's prime minister Winston Churchill, and Soviet dictator Joseph Stalin, divided Germany into four occupation zones. The United States, Great Britain, the Soviet Union, and France would oversee the demilitarization, reconstructing, and so-called denazification of German society. They also discussed the partitioning of Europe that led to Stalin's acquiring control of Poland, Romania, Czechoslovakia, Hungary, and Bulgaria—the Soviet-dominated Eastern Bloc.

Our national interest does not allow standing between East and West. Germany needs cooperation with the West and understanding with the East.
—WILLY BRANDT

Five hundred thousand West Germans attend a memorial service in West Berlin for those killed by Soviet forces in East Berlin on June 16, 1953, during an uprising against Soviet occupation. Brandt believed that this unrest encouraged the Soviets to tighten their grip on the East German communist government and its Socialist Unity party (SED).

In February 1945 the leaders of the Allied nations met in Yalta, in the Soviet Union, to discuss Europe's political status after the Nazis' eventual defeat. From left to right are: British prime minister Winston Churchill, U.S. president Franklin D. Roosevelt, and Soviet dictator Joseph Stalin.

By 1946 Brandt was eager to return to Germany. He persuaded several Swedish newspapers to send him back to his homeland as their correspondent at the Nuremberg war trials. The trials, held in Nuremberg where Hitler once presided over gigantic Nazi rallies, brought the surviving high-level Nazi leaders before the International War Crimes Tribunal.

Brandt was one of the few Germans permitted by the Allies to cover the trial. For 11 months Brandt heard the most horrifying crimes of the Nazi regime revealed. Nevertheless, he was not convinced that justice was always impartially administered. He expressed his doubts about the trial in a book entitled *Criminals and Other Germans*, originally published in Scandinavia.

Brandt left Nuremberg before the trials were concluded in order to attend the first postwar convention of the Social Democratic party in May 1946. He served in a dual capacity as journalist and delegate representing both the newspaper *Arbeiderbladet* and the Norwegian Labor party.

Kurt Schumacher was elected chairman of the Social Democratic party. Schumacher was a tough-talking nationalist and anticommunist, who had

Germany After World War II and During the Cold War

FINLAND

NORWAY

• Leningrad

SWEDEN

ESTONIA

SOVIET UNION

NORTH SEA

LATVIA

DENMARK

LITHUANIA

BALTIC SEA

• Berlin

EAST GERMANY
(German Democratic
Republic)

POLAND

• Bonn

BELGIUM

Luxemburg

WEST GERMANY
(Federal Republic
of Germany)

CZECHOSLOVAKIA

FRANCE

• Vienna

SWITZERLAND

HUNGARY

ROMANIA

ITALY

YUGOSLAVIA

BLACK
SEA

ADRIATIC
SEA

BULGARIA

ALBANIA

GREECE

U.S. Zone	
British Zone	
French Zone	
Soviet-dominated Eastern Bloc Nations	
Soviet Union	

After World War II, Germany lost eastern territories to Poland and the Soviet Union and became two nations: the Federal Republic of Germany (West Germany) and German Democratic Republic (East Germany). Inside Soviet-dominated East Germany, noncommunist West Berlin, and communist East Berlin became a crucible of cold war conflict.

Herman Göring, head of the Nazi *Luftwaffe* (air force) and a top-ranking official in Hitler's government, testifies before the War Crimes Tribunal, held in Nuremberg in 1946. Still a Norwegian citizen, Brandt attended the trials as a reporter.

spent all but a few months of the Nazis' 12-year dictatorship in concentration camps. In his acceptance speech, Schumacher took a hard line against any Soviet presence in his nation. Schumacher's combative attitude toward the Soviets did not particularly appeal to Brandt, however. In the meantime, many prominent Social Democrats were maneuvering for political positions in occupied Germany. Brandt was now eager to enter this new political arena. When the Allied occupation forces withdrew, these leaders would be ready to steer a course for the new German government. It was not long before the party sought out Brandt. Several important political and nonpolitical positions, ranging from director of the German press corps to mayor of Lübeck, were offered to him. None of these could lure him away from his journalistic work in Norway, however. Curiously, it was an assignment from the Norwegian government that finally propelled Brandt into German politics. In December 1946 he was appointed Norwegian press attaché. In January 1947, he reported to the Norwegian Foreign Office in Berlin to begin work. When he arrived in Berlin, Brandt was shocked by what he saw — a city in ruins.

In the 50 years prior to the Nazi takeover, Berlin had been one of Europe's most cosmopolitan cities, a center of commerce, culture, and ideas. Always a stronghold of socialists, the city had staunchly opposed the Nazi bid for power, and did not capitulate to Hitler's regime until the Reichstag was burned in 1933. As the nerve center of the Nazi regime, Berlin was bombed so heavily by the Allies in the final weeks of World War II that one-third of its buildings were blasted into rubble. When Brandt arrived in the city in 1947, the United States and the Soviet Union, former allies whose combined forces vanquished Hitler's Germany, now squared off against each other. From the ashes of World War II there emerged a conflict between the victors that fell just short of open warfare. This was the cold war, involving espionage, propaganda, and an arms race.

Children play in the rubble as workers clear debris in Berlin after World War II. In an effort to rebuild a Europe crippled by six years of war, in 1947 the United States undertook the Marshall Plan, which sharply curtailed Soviet influence. Brandt recalled in the late 1980s that the Soviets "saw all the fish swimming out of their nets."

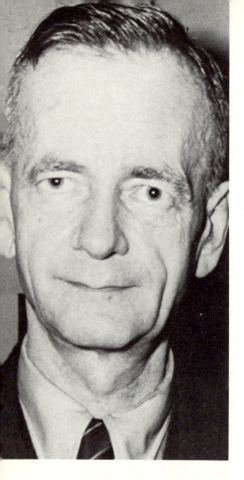

Kurt Schumacher, chairman of the Social Democratic party, spent 12 years in Nazi concentration camps. Brandt disagreed with many of the chairman's policies, but Schumacher nonetheless appointed Brandt his representative in Berlin in 1948.

In the meantime, Brandt remained a German-born Norwegian citizen, living in Germany and working for the Norwegian government. For months after his arrival in Berlin Brandt wrestled with an important decision. While German Social Democratic officials were trying to win him back, he was forced to decide whether or not to remain a Norwegian citizen living in Germany; an alien in his own country.

In January 1948, Schumacher offered to make Brandt his executive representative in Berlin, an offer Brandt could not easily turn down. Working closely with Schumacher would immediately place Brandt in a position of prominence within Germany's revitalized Social Democratic party. Brandt wanted to bring about within the party what he called "constructive reformism." Brandt had come to admire Berlin's citizens for their stolid determination to rebuild. He wanted to remain there and participate in the reconstruction of Germany. It was also clear to him that Berlin was at the center of the global contest between the Soviet Union and the noncommunist Western nations led by the United States. While in Europe at this time the writer Janet Flanner noted in her book *Paris Journal, 1944–65*, "The USSR and USA areas of influence are expanding. It is as if Europe were slowly entering a new ice age."

Brandt accepted Schumacher's offer, sending off one last report to Oslo four days later. Schumacher then used his influence to restore German citizenship to "Herbert Ernst Karl Frahm — also called Willy Brandt." Not until 1949 would Frahm legally change his name to Willy Brandt.

Movement by Allied personnel between Berlin and the Western occupation zones of Germany was guaranteed by the Potsdam Declaration signed in August 1945 by U.S. president Harry S. Truman, Soviet dictator Joseph Stalin, and Clement Attlee, who succeeded Winston Churchill as British prime minister. Until about 1947 the Soviet Union allowed noncommunist parties to operate in the Eastern European nations they occupied. Governments

called national fronts, with help from Social Democratic parties, tried to rebuild and reform their
countries. By 1948, however, the communists had
tightened their grip in the Soviet zone of Berlin and
the rest of Soviet-occupied Germany. In February
the communists in Czechoslovakia took over the
government. Brandt again attracted attention with
a blistering attack on the coup in Czechoslovakia:
"If that which took place in Prague [Czechoslova-
kia's capital] is supposed to embody socialism, then
we have nothing more to do with that socialism."
The United States, Britain, and France had already
been instrumental in reestablishing local government in the three Western zones of occupation. In
the Soviet-occupied Eastern zone, the Socialist Unity party, or SED, adopted a draft for a new German
constitution under the watchful eye of Soviet authorities. The SED was formed when Social Democrats and communists in Soviet-occupied East
Berlin were consolidated. (German communist Walter Ulbricht, who had been in Moscow from 1938
until the war's end, oversaw this merger.) This party
also asked the Western occupation forces to allow a
popular vote in the three zones and in Berlin concerning this constitution. Because the Soviet-
backed Socialist Unity party was dominating East
Germany, as well as the constitutional initiative, the

Brandt speaks to a Social Democratic party convention in Berlin on August 5, 1949. Though he gave up his Norwegian citizenship in 1948, Brandt still felt a strong attachment to that country. Rut, his wife until 1978, was Norwegian.

Citizens of West Berlin watch "Operation Vittles" in action as an American transport plane prepares to land in their besieged city. West Berlin's more than 2 million people were cut off by the Soviets from food and supplies during the Berlin blockade (1948—49). Brandt helped organize the Berlin airlift, which counteracted the blockade.

Western nations refused. Instead, on June 1, 1948, the Western powers adopted the London Agreement, which authorized the Germans living in those zones to draft their own constitution.

The Soviets were furious when their constitution, which permitted only a one-party political system, was rejected. They proceeded to accuse the Western allies of attempting to seize control of the Western zones. By the middle of June, communication between the West and Soviet-dominated Eastern Europe had broken down completely.

On June 20, 1948, under the U.S.-administered Marshall Plan for European reconstruction, West Germans exchanged their old reichsmarks for a new currency, the *deutsche mark*. The following day, Soviet occupation forces blockaded all traffic between West Berlin and West Germany. Food supplies, coal, and electrical power to West Berlin were cut off. It would only be a matter of weeks, the Soviets reasoned, before Western authorities met their demand for a constitutional referendum.

As Schumacher's representative in Berlin, Brandt found himself caught up in a potentially explosive event. If the Berlin blockade was not lifted, food and medical supplies would be exhausted. If the ensuing panic and fear generated serious unrest, or even riots, the Soviets could find reason to intervene with troops under the guise of protecting their interests in East Berlin. Brandt and Ernst Reuter, a popular city councillor recently elected in the United States occupied zone, met with United States officials, who indicated it might be possible to bring supplies by airplane to Berlin.

Five days after the Berlin blockade began, the Allies responded with "Operation Vittles," the famed Berlin airlift. The first day's delivery was made by 32 transport planes carrying 120 tons of food and supplies. During the next 11 months of the blockade, which lasted until May 1949, nearly 1,600,000 tons of food, clothing, medicine, coal, and other vital supplies were flown into the city.

The Soviets misjudged the citizens of West Berlin. Instead of being demoralized, they found a new sense of solidarity and common purpose from enduring the Berlin blockade. The Berlin airlift gave the city its first victory since the devastation inflicted by World War II.

His organization of the Berlin airlift earned Brandt the affection of Berlin's citizenry that was to endure throughout his political career. Brandt and Reuter, who was elected West Berlin's first mayor in June 1949, set the groundwork for Brandt's own successful career in the city. Brandt had seen Berlin through its first major crisis since World War II. Berlin, beleaguered as it was, had become Brandt's home in Germany. In August the Christian Democratic Union, the leading conservative party, led by Konrad Adenauer, gained a majority in the West German parliament, which was divided into the *Bundestag*, the lower house, and *Bundesrat*, the upper house. Adenauer, who was once mayor of Cologne and had been imprisoned by Hitler, became federal chancellor. The Social Democrats were reeling from these defeats.

Brandt made Berlin glitter. He gave it a role for the young.
—HERBERT WEHNER
Brandt political associate

During the airlift, efforts to unify Germany were at a standstill, with the Western powers and the Soviets unable to reach any agreement. When it became clear that the Soviet blockade had failed, negotiations broke off completely. On May 23, 1949, 11 days after the Soviets lifted the Berlin blockade, German territory formerly occupied by the United States, Great Britain, and France became the Federal Republic of Germany, or West Germany.

The Soviets had made a serious effort through propaganda and diplomatic channels to prevent a noncommunist West German state. On October 7, 1949, three days after Brandt's first son, Peter, was born, the German Democratic Republic (DDR) was established in East Germany. Its constitution, originally drafted by the Soviet-oriented Socialist Unity party in March 1948, was declared effective.

Insurgents head toward Budapest, the Hungarian capital, in November 1956. After the Soviet-dominated regime ruthlessly smashed the Hungarian revolt, Brandt rushed to the border of West and East Berlin to defuse a possible confrontation between West Berliners and Soviet troops.

Willy Brandt resigned his post as Social Democratic representative to Berlin in 1950 and was appointed Berlin's representative to the West German parliament by mayor Ernst Reuter. Brandt became known—to his displeasure—as "Reuter's man." His thinking was indeed closest to that of Reuter's, who wanted a Social Democratic party that was practical, not hemmed in by theory. Though he was critical of the pro-Western Adenauer, Brandt thought Schumacher's nationalist hope for a united Germany was too extreme. For the next several years, Brandt shuttled back and forth between Berlin, still the capital, and Bonn, in North Rhine-Westphalia, which became the actual seat of the new West German government.

In 1952 Brandt boldly challenged Franz Neumann, the current Berlin SPD chairman, for the Social Democratic chairmanship, but in doing so Brandt jumped the gun. Neumann, rather than Brandt, enjoyed Schumacher's backing, and Brandt was easily defeated by his opponent. Tensions between East and West Germany and the political repression resulting from East Germany's one-party Communist state triggered rioting in East Berlin on June 17, 1953. When Soviet tanks rolled down Alexanderplatz, East Berlin's main boulevard, and opened fire on stone-throwing rioters, some 25 East Germans were killed. Approximately 600 more were executed for their role in the rebellion.

The quick suppression of the uprising in East Berlin displayed the Soviets' intentions to snuff out any resistance in Eastern Europe with military force. This policy prompted worldwide outrage when 8,000 people were killed as Soviet armored forces and anti-Soviet rebels clashed in the streets of Budapest, Hungary, in November 1956.

When news of the killings in Budapest reached West Berlin, tens of thousands took to the streets, storming north toward the Brandenburg Gate, a magnificent public entryway built in the late 18th century, now at the border between East and West Berlin. Brandt was alarmed when he received word of the large and potentially violent crowd. Might not

> *In all this wheeling and dealing we Berliners don't want to be an object of barter . . . Look upon this city and realize that you dare not give away this people.*
> —ERNST REUTER
> mayor of West Berlin, on Western Allies' policy toward the city

The Berlin Wall winds toward the Brandenburg Gate at the center of the city. By the summer of 1961, four years after Brandt became mayor of West Berlin, refugees from Soviet-occupied East Berlin were fleeing westward across the border at a rate of 3,000 people per day. The wall was built by the Soviets to prevent this exodus.

the Soviets in East Berlin use the demonstration as an excuse to launch a bloody offensive into West Berlin?

Without hesitation Brandt and his wife, Rut, sped through the streets and reached the mob just a few blocks from the East Berlin border. From there, Brandt could see the Soviet occupation forces waiting, armed with automatic rifles, and supported by the now-infamous Soviet tanks. Using a policeman's megaphone, Brandt pleaded with the crowd to remain calm and stay inside the Western sector to avoid confrontation with Soviet and East German troops. Although in no mood for compromise, the restless mob gradually came to a halt. But they refused to be dispersed. Standing atop a police car in front of the Brandenburg Gate, Brandt realized that the next gunshot or insult shouted at the mob from behind him in East Berlin could trigger a worse riot than the Soviets had already crushed in their own zone.

To divert the mob's attention, Brandt began singing the German national anthem through his megaphone, *"Deutschland, Deutschland über alles."* ("Germany, Germany over all.") Gradually a few groups of voices joined his, until finally thousands of men and women were singing in unison, filling the cold November air and drowning out the rumbling motors of the Soviet tanks less than 100 yards away. Brandt's courage and quick thinking defused a potentially disastrous situation and solidified his popularity with the citizens of West Berlin. He later waved aside praise for this act with the offhand comment that "in any political situation it is useful to know that my German countrymen are fond of singing."

On September 30, 1957, Berlin's Social Democratic representatives elected Brandt overwhelmingly as Berlin's *Regierende Bürgermeister*, or governing mayor, to fill the vacancy created by the death in August of Dr. Otto Suhr, who had also been president of Berlin's House of Representatives. Three days later Brandt won a special election held by the House of Representatives to complete Suhr's term. In 1958 Brandt was reelected by a majority to his first full term in office.

Brandt (left), as governing mayor of West Berlin, confers with West Germany's first chancellor, Konrad Adenauer, in 1959. An avid anticommunist, Adenauer nevertheless neglected West Berlin's plight inside East Germany and lost control of the West German parliament in 1961.

Herbert Wehner, a former communist who joined the Social Democrats in 1946, became closely associated with Brandt as a deputy chairman of the SPD. As vice-chairman of the SPD, Wehner was sometimes considered the mastermind behind the party.

In November 1959 the Social Democrats decided to formulate a new program for their party. This was to be the Godesberg Program. The fundamental issue concerned what should be done about Marxist principles in the party — especially as the cold war intensified. Marxism would have to be made less important to the party's principles, if not dropped entirely. At this secret meeting Herbert Wehner spoke in favor of helping the SPD to make a breakthrough by opening the party to as many different points of view as possible. Brandt agreed. In this way, the Social Democrats could show that they were responsible enough to govern. Wehner became a leading figure in the SPD, which he had joined in 1946, and both he and Brandt were elected deputy chairmen of the party in 1962. Brandt had first encountered Wehner in Paris in 1936 while trying to organize an anti-Nazi underground. Though Wehner was expelled from the German Communist party in 1942, he had been in Moscow from 1939 until 1941. Long associated with one another, Wehner and Brandt were very different in temperament.

Their partnership, which was to last for many years, was often stormy.

During this period between 1949 and 1960, taking advantage of the freedom of movement within the city, more than 2,500,000 East Germans crossed the border into West Berlin and did not return. By the summer of 1961 the number of refugees crossing into West Berlin exceeded 3,000 each day — until construction of the Berlin Wall began. East Berliners began this bright Sunday as they had become accustomed, streaming to the sector borders to visit friends and relatives in the West. Along the autobahn, the recently completed highways, begun under Hitler's regime and connecting East Germany and West Berlin, they encountered a series of recently planted barriers. At some points travelers were even threatened by gun-toting East German soldiers and forced to turn back.

For weeks Brandt had been protesting the gradual appearance of these barriers, and the increased hostility of the border guards between East and West Berlin. The Western Allies, however, refused to voice disapproval to the government of Soviet premier and Communist party chairman Nikita Khrushchev. Since 1958, when the West rejected his demand for the creation of a "demilitarized free city" in West Berlin, Khrushchev had hinted that the "outdated" arrangement between East and West Berlin could be corrected through military force. Because the Western Allies were determined to remain in West Berlin at any cost, this threat created the Berlin crisis — the possibility of military action between the United States, the Soviet Union, and their allies. A tense silence had settled over East and West Berlin.

On August 16, East German construction workers began laying the brick and mortar of what was to become the Berlin Wall. Brandt, who had been campaigning in West Germany for Social Democratic candidates in the upcoming national elections, hurried back to West Berlin to observe the crisis. Urgent telegrams were sent to other Western leaders, including John F. Kennedy, who had been elected president of the United States in 1960. Still, the Western Allies did not react.

Marx, Engels, Bebel, La Salle and Bernstein, the revered party . . . fathers, had to make room for a modern political pluralistic community of common will and values.
—VIOLA HERMS DRATH
German historian, on the
Godesberg Program

Brandt appeared before the West German parliament, demanding that steps be taken against the Soviets beyond the usual formal protests. But Adenauer refused to acknowledge any crisis at all. Adenauer hoped the trouble in Berlin would reflect badly on Brandt's Social Democrats in the upcoming elections.

With every passing day the wall was growing higher and thicker. Chairman Ulbricht of East Germany's Communist party, who had also been the first secretary of the SED, referred to it as his "anti-Fascist protective wall." More accurately, the wall was not built to protect the people of East Berlin but to prevent them from escaping the communist regime. This became blatantly evident when machine guns were placed atop the newly built East German watchtowers. These weapons pointed inward *toward* East Berlin's own citizens.

Adenauer finally came to Berlin nine days after the wall was begun. Brandt was so furious with what seemed to him to be Adenauer's stalling and manipulations that he had to be persuaded by fellow Social Democrats to shake the chancellor's hand after he arrived at the airport. (Brandt was also angered by Adenauer's repeated references to him as "Herr Frahm.")

As the crisis progressed, Kennedy sent Brandt a message meant to assure the Germans that the U.S. perception of the crisis was changing. But Kennedy firmly ruled out any U.S. military action. Clearly, Brandt and his embattled city would have to stand alone.

When the Berlin Wall reached completion in late August 1961, so did the tragedy of Berlin as a divided city. Hopes that the Western Allies would solve the question of a divided Germany were over. Brandt was now convinced that German politicians would have to develop solutions to Germany's problems by themselves. Germany could no longer rely solely on the United States and its allies.

Brandt was still able to turn Berlin's loss into a gain for the Social Democrats. Adenauer's high-handed refusal to come to Brandt's assistance back-

Walter Ulbricht led East Germany (the German Democratic Republic) from 1950 until his death in 1973. A member of the German Communist party since 1918, he had close ties to the Soviet Union and organized the Socialist Unity party, which drafted the East German Constitution.

fired on the Christian Democrats. On September 17, 1961, Adenauer and the Christian Democrats narrowly won reelection, but lost majority control of the West German parliament. The Free Democrats gained 12.7 percent of the vote — an unusually large percentage for that party. With newfound strength in the West German parliament, Brandt suggested to Adenauer that he create a coalition government of all parties — a "big coalition." Such a coalition's time would eventually come — though not yet — between the Christian Democrats, the Social Democrats, and the Free Democrats.

For the moment, Willy Brandt was "the best known mayor in the world," as one newspaper put it. Brandt's experience in Berlin set him on a road that would eventually lead to the chancellor's office in Bonn.

Newlyweds in West Berlin peer over the Berlin Wall into East Berlin to greet relatives separated from them by the barrier built in 1961. East German communist leader Ulbricht called the concrete and barbed-wire structure an "anti-Fascist protective wall." In fact, West Germans had feared that East Germany would try to absorb West Berlin.

7

Chancellor As Peacemaker

By the early 1960s, Willy Brandt had become a political phenomenon. His popularity in Berlin was at its peak, and in 1962 Brandt was reelected as mayor. In the first months of his second term Brandt invited U.S. president Kennedy to visit Berlin during his June tour of West Germany. Brandt and his staff had made sure that there would be a good turnout. But even they were surprised by the size of the crowd that gathered to greet Kennedy.

Kennedy closed his short speech by saying that 2,000 years before, it had been the proudest claim to say, "I am a citizen of Rome." Now the president said that the proudest phrase of the free world was "I am a Berliner."

"Therefore as a free man," Kennedy declared to the crowd of thousands gathered less than three miles from the wall itself, "I am proud to say *Ich bin ein Berliner*!"

When the crowd heard Kennedy intone these words their cheers could be heard across the city. Brandt shared in the overwhelming success of his distinguished guest's speech, and later referred to Kennedy's visit as "the great day for Berlin."

We do not seek admirers. We need critical people to think with us, decide with us, to take responsibility with us.
—WILLY BRANDT
on a democracy's needs

Brandt addresses a conference in Bad Godesberg in February 1964, when he was elected chairman of the Social Democratic party. The following year, Brandt became the Social Democratic candidate for chancellor. First elected governing mayor of West Berlin in 1957, he was reelected in 1958 and 1963.

U.S. president John F. Kennedy, Mayor Brandt, and Chancellor Adenauer ride through a shower of confetti in West Berlin, during the president's visit in June 1963. Although he ruled out confronting the Soviets over West Berlin's ordeal, Kennedy won immense popularity, telling the city's citizens *"Ich bin ein Berliner."* ("I am a Berliner.")

In February 1964 Brandt was elected chairman of the Social Democratic party, succeeding Erich Ollenhauer, and in 1965 headed the party's national ticket as candidate for chancellor, challenging the incumbent, Ludwig Erhard. Erhard had been appointed chancellor by the West German parliament following the aging Adenauer's resignation in 1963. Although he lacked Adenauer's strength of character, Erhard was a difficult man to dislike. A thickset man with white hair, German voters perceived Erhard as the very picture of the prosperous German and kindly father figure. When early polls showed that many conservative Germans took the view that Brandt was an upstart, spoiling for a fight with the Soviets in Berlin, Erhard's Christian Democrats decided to attack Brandt personally. Avoiding a discussion of the issues whenever possible, the conservatives focused solely on image. Beside Erhard's reassuring appearance, Brandt appeared to be a young tough with a questionable background.

Brandt refused to counter these charges with similar attacks against Erhard. Even mainstream conservatives and Erhard himself attempted to distance themselves from the viciousness of these tactics. Nevertheless, the damage was done. The "dirty campaign," as it was soon called, had captured the attention of the press and public. It was debated, denounced, or enjoyed. In the ensuing commotion, Brandt was unable to focus the election on the issues. After an exhausting campaign, in which he gave 550 speeches, victory went to his opponent.

Brandt was hurt by what he considered a crushing defeat. Erhard won 47.6 percent of the 32 million votes cast; Brandt received 39.3 percent. The election, however, was not the disaster Brandt felt it to be. The Social Democrats had gained more than 1 million votes since the last national election. Brandt, however, would not be consoled.

Brandt speaks with Christian Democrat Ludwig Erhard, October 1961. In 1965, during Brandt's campaign for chancellor, the CDU cast doubt upon Brandt's name change and accused him of being loyal to a foreign government (Norway).

"I am not going to be a candidate for chancellor in the 1969 election," Brandt, saddened and resentful over his defeats, told party officials after the election. "Do your own dirty work." Many of his Social Democratic comrades feared he would withdraw entirely from politics — perhaps even return to Norway.

Despite these political setbacks, Brandt found great comfort and support in his private life. He remained happily married to Rut, who stood by his side throughout a difficult campaign. She seemed to endure the personal attacks with more grace than her husband. Although Brandt was often away from home for long periods attending to the incessant demands of his political life, he was a devoted father to his children: Peter, born in 1949, Lars, born in 1951, and Matthias, born a decade later. In addition, Brandt regularly saw his daughter, Ninja, who visited often from Norway where she had remained after Brandt's divorce from her mother, Carlota. Brandt took delight in his children's antics and activities. He was eager to hear of what they were doing even if his responsibilities did not allow him to always actively participate. He also took grave offense whenever their behavior was publicly criticized.

Günter Grass, the German novelist, best known for his novels *The Tin Drum* and *The Flounder*, invited Brandt's oldest sons, Peter and Lars, to play small roles in the film of his best-selling *Cat and Mouse*. Peter, then 17, already considered himself something of a radical leftist, and it pleased him to be in a film that ridiculed German militarism. The conservative press promptly accused Brandt of indulging his sons at the expense of patriotism. Officials of his own party privately criticized Brandt for permitting his sons to accept Grass's offer.

"The kids wanted to perform in a movie and I didn't want to say no," Brandt responded. But when one official further suggested that his sons had become a "burden for the party and should be sent to private school in Switzerland," Brandt became incensed.

"You can decide that if you want," he said firmly. "But if you put the choice to me between being a

father and being Party Chairman, you will have a new Party Chairman. The choice, for me, is easy." No mention was made of the film or of Peter and Lars again.

A year and a half after his victory at the polls, Ludwig Erhard's government was in serious crisis. Although Erhard's Christian Democrats had won the election, his campaign's efforts to personally discredit Brandt had left the party divided. Erhard was chancellor, but his ability to lead was damaged. When Erhard presented his second national budget with a projected deficit of 5 billion Deutsche Marks (equivalent to roughly $1.5 billion dollars), and proposed substantial tax increases, a majority of Christian Democrats refused to support him. Cabinet members quit in protest. Soon Erhard's administration collapsed.

Brandt's sons Lars (left) and Peter (third from left) with novelist Günter Grass, who asked them to act in the film version of his novel Cat and Mouse. When Brandt did not stop his sons from working with the leftist Grass, he drew criticism from fellow Social Democrats.

On a visit to Poland in December 1970, Chancellor Brandt solemnly kneels in front of a memorial to the Jewish rebels massacred by the Nazis during the Warsaw Ghetto uprising. Brandt succeeded Kiesinger as West German chancellor in 1969 when Social Democrats, in a coalition with the Free Democratic party, won 48.5 percent of the vote in parliament.

Meanwhile, behind the scenes, a political bargain had been struck between Brandt and Kurt Georg Kiesinger, a 62-year-old member of what remained of the Great Coalition. Considered a foreign affairs expert, Kiesinger had also been a Nazi — a member of Hitler's foreign ministry headed by Joachim von Ribbentrop, who was executed for war crimes in 1946. On November 26, 1966, these unlikely allies announced their agreement to head a new government with Kiesinger as chancellor and Brandt serving as vice-chancellor and foreign minister. This became known as the "Grand Coalition." This was a valuable opportunity for the Social Democrats to prove that they were *regierungsfähig* — capable of governing. Brandt and Kiesinger toasted each other and smiled into the press's cameras. Brandt, unbeknownst to newspaper readers, had stood on a suitcase for photographs of the two leaders to make himself seem as tall as the imposing Kiesinger. It was to prove an unfortunate mismatch.

As foreign minister Brandt was in the international limelight again, which he clearly enjoyed. That year, Brandt published his collected papers from his days in exile, entitled *Draussen* (*Outside*). For the next three years he traveled continually. He called on French president Charles de Gaulle in an effort to strengthen ties between Bonn and Paris, initiated dialogue with Romanian and Hungarian officials, and conferred with President Lyndon Johnson about U.S.-German relations and the continued presence of American troops in Western Europe.

Kiesinger, however, still grappling with the economic problems left by Erhard's administration, ruthlessly undercut much of his foreign minister's efforts. Angered by Brandt's successful talks with de Gaulle, Kiesinger visited Paris himself, only to find de Gaulle aloof and vague. After months of delicate negotiations between the United States and the Soviet Union about limiting worldwide production of nuclear weapons, Kiesinger publicly complained that the two superpowers were creating an "atomic confederacy" for themselves. This remark so enraged President Johnson that Kiesinger was pressured into apologizing.

Chancellor Brandt talks with Leonid Brezhnev, general secretary of the Communist party, while visiting the Soviet Union in September 1971. By signing the Moscow Treaty in 1970, Brandt inaugurated *Ostpolitik* (Eastern Policy) thus recognizing the borders of Eastern European nations under Soviet domination since the end of World War II.

Brandt meets with East German minister president Willi Stoph in Erfurt, East Germany, on March 19, 1970, a meeting the East German called a "turning point" in relations between their two nations. Since the formation of the two Germanys following World War II, the West had refused to recognize the East.

Although Kiesinger's inept attempts to control West Germany's foreign policy infuriated Brandt, he was largely unable to do anything about the problem. He had to swallow his anger and publicly support Kiesinger. West Germany could not afford another collapse of its government. For the next three years, both men continued to exasperate each other as their political alliance became increasingly unstable.

As the national elections of 1969 approached, Brandt wasted little time disassociating himself from Kiesinger. Because of his relative success as foreign minister, he had recovered from his defeat in the 1965 election. Brandt approached this campaign for the chancellor's office with unusual confidence and good cheer. On September 28, 1969, the Social Democrats, led by Willy Brandt, won a majority with 48.5 percent of the vote. After two decades of lapping at the heels of a dominant Christian Democratic party, the Social Democrats were the majority party in West Germany's government. As chancellor, Willy Brandt felt confident that he could give the majority of voters the kind of government they demanded.

Brandt's Social Democrats soon wielded most of the power in a coalition with the Free Democrats, who were content to restrain reformism at home while allowing Brandt's party free reign in foreign policy. East Germany marked its 20th anniversary on October 7, 1969. Soviet Communist party chairman Leonid Brezhnev visited East Berlin during the political festivities with the clear purpose of sending a friendly signal to the newly elected Brandt. The Soviet leadership was uneasy with Brandt's victory. They were still wary of Brandt, who had demonstrated his skill at foreign policy during the Berlin airlift and through positive relations with Kennedy.

East German officials were concerned with Brandt's ascent to power. Soon after being sworn in as chancellor, Brandt flew to Berlin to visit his old constituents. As expected by officials in both West and East Berlin, his reception was tumultuous. East Germany's foreign ministry accused Brandt "of endangering peace and security" with his visit. Nevertheless, Brandt's formidable reputation in foreign policy caused Communist party secretary Walter Ulbricht to soften his previous hard-line demand that West Germany establish diplomatic recognition of the German Democratic Republic. After Brandt's installation as chancellor, Ulbricht suggested a treaty between East and West Germany that would simply acknowledge the existence of the two Germanys, thus easing nearly 25 years of discord. Brandt had campaigned with the single theme of "building peace." Once elected, he quickly set out to fulfill his promise.

Brandt's first move was toward the West. Following intensive preparations, the chancellor traveled to the Hague, the capital of the Netherlands, to participate in a high-level conference of the European Economic Community (EEC), better known as the Common Market. The EEC was established in 1957 by the Treaty of Rome, signed by France, West Germany, Italy, Belgium, the Netherlands, and Luxembourg, and is dedicated to increasing European economic productivity and integration. The Common Market was meant to remove trade barriers and coordinate and integrate the economic policies of

> *The end of the blackmail started in 1969 when Brandt said Germany was governed by Germans who had been liberated, not conquered.*
> —HORST EHMKE
> SPD official

89

member nations. Despite these noble internationalist goals, the Common Market began to stagnate by 1970. Although in less than 10 years trade between Germany and France increased by 40 percent, France still refused trade relations with certain nations, such as Great Britain. At the Common Market summit, French president Georges Pompidou again refused Britain's request for entry, claiming that Britain's inclusion might weaken some Common Market members. Although the words were not spoken, it was well known that France had become uneasy with West Germany's newfound economic prosperity.

Brandt shrewdly addressed Pompidou's remarks in his own speech. "Those who fear the economic strength of West Germany, Brandt replied, "should favor expansion," subtly suggesting that if the French were truly concerned about West German economic growth, they should perhaps form a trade partnership with Great Britain. Pompidou reversed France's traditional stance and agreed to Britain's inclusion.

Brandt's successful efforts to open the Common Market to other European nations, including the Republic of Ireland, Denmark, and Norway, became known as his *Westpolitik*, or "Western Policy." But it was creating *Ostpolitik*, or "Eastern Policy," that earned Brandt the respect of Western leaders as well as closer ties to West Germany's foreign adversaries to the East — the Warsaw Pact nations and the Soviets. The foundation of Brandt's Ostpolitik was his negotiation of "renunciation of force" pacts with the Soviet Union, Poland, and most importantly, East Germany. The Moscow Treaty was the cornerstone of these agreements to mutually recognize post–World War II boundaries. These agreements effectively became the peace treaties formally ending World War II on the Eastern front. Brandt's substantial success in negotiating peaceful relations with former foes resulted from complex diplomatic maneuvers abroad and promoting a fundamental rethinking of traditional politics at home.

Brandt's Ostpolitik led to the first official meetings between himself and the leaders of East Germany. A "renunciation of force" pact agreed to by West Germany and the Soviet Union was signed in August of 1970, declaring mutual respect for "the territorial integrity" of existing European nations. Three years later, Brandt agreed to abandon all claims made under the Munich Settlement by Hitler's government in 1938. By doing so Brandt gave up any West German claims on Czechoslovakian territory. On December 7, 1970, Brandt traveled to Warsaw, the Polish capital, to sign the agreement acknowledging Poland's postwar annexation of 40,000 square miles of former German territory. Before the agreement was signed, Brandt captured the attention of the world with an unexpected and powerfully emotional gesture.

Brandt laid a wreath at Poland's Tomb of the Unknown Soldier, and then went with another wreath to Warsaw's memorial to the Jewish ghetto. The ghetto became the site of a resistance movement against the Nazi occupiers in 1944. Standing before the simple granite slab commemorating the 500,000 Polish Jews murdered by the Nazis, Brandt impulsively fell to his knees after silently placing a wreath before the monument. Brandt appeared to be asking forgiveness for Germany's past wrongdoing from those who suffered the crimes and atrocities perpetrated by Nazi occupiers. This gesture was eloquent in that it did much to show Brandt's — and his nation's — genuine remorse for those who suffered and died as a direct result of Germany's Nazi past.

Finally, after much negotiation, diplomatic maneuvering, and arguing within Brandt's own government, Ostpolitik established the basis of a new relationship between East and West Germany. Reversing Bonn's previous policy, Brandt devised the formula of "two German states within one German nation." This facilitated a reconciliation — short of full diplomatic recognition — between the two Germanys. More importantly, it was the first step in easing the standoff between East and West Europe. Brandt met with East German premier Willi Stoph (who succeeded Walter Ulbricht in 1971), and proclaimed, "The Germans must be at peace with them-

Israeli prime minister Golda Meir greets West German chancellor Brandt upon his arrival in Tel Aviv, June 7, 1973. The visit stirred controversy in Israel, because Brandt represented a nation whose rule by the Nazis from 1933 to 1945 resulted in the Holocaust — the systematic murder of 6 million European Jews.

selves, so that the world can be at peace with Germany." That year, *Time* magazine named the West German chancellor its "Man of the Year."

Brandt received an even greater honor the following year, however. For his efforts to remove the hostility between the two nations and to promote peaceful relations, Brandt was awarded the Nobel Peace Prize in 1971.

First presented in 1901, the Nobel Peace Prize was named after the Swedish inventor Alfred B. Nobel, who had devoted his energies to creating a more effective means to wage war — the explosive dynamite. Nobel left his considerable fortune to establish this prestigious award, also given in the fields of literature, physics, chemistry, medicine and, since 1968, economics. Brandt joined the ranks of such fellow Peace Prize laureates as U.S. president Woodrow Wilson (1919), American social worker Jane Addams (1931), Dr. Albert Schweitzer (1952), and American civil-rights activist Reverend Martin Luther King, Jr. (1964).

In the days preceding the final decision of the Nobel committee, if Brandt had thought he was being considered for the Peace Prize, he did not mention it. German press reporters, however, speculated that Brandt had been "short-listed," meaning that he was one of only a few being seriously considered. After reviewing 39 nominations, Brandt was unanimously chosen as peace laureate from an impressive collection of names. The news that he had been awarded the Nobel Prize by the Norwegian Storting first reached the chancellor's office on October 20, 1971. Brandt was hard at work. Hunched over his desk, Brandt refused to interrupt his work to comment on the unofficial announcement of the award.

When the telegram finally arrived, formally announcing that he was the award's recipient, Brandt appeared moderately pleased, but also somewhat embarrassed. Public reaction was overwhelming. Telegrams and letters poured in from around the world, from heads of state and schoolchildren alike. Political differences were held in check as the German people looked upon Brandt with pride and gratitude, not only as the winner of a prestigious award, but also as a leader singled out as an outstanding worker for peace. A member of the conservative Christian Democratic Union (CDU) complained to a reporter soon after the award was announced, "How can you campaign against a man who is suddenly billed as 'the Peace Chancellor'?" Indeed, the West German parliament unanimously offered congratulations, although as Brandt wryly noted, "Perhaps my party colleagues were slightly more pleased than the rest."

That night a torchlight procession arrived at Brandt's home in Bonn's residential Venusberg district. Outside, the cheers of hundreds of young people filled the autumn air as their flames peacefully glimmered in the night. Thirty-five years earlier uniformed Nazis had marched in torchlit ceremonies, feverishly chanting nationalist slogans, and burning books they considered unfit to be read by citizens of Hitler's Reich. When asked once how he

In Nuremberg, West Germany, young demonstrators are doused by police water cannons in 1969. Often sympathetic to young people's opinions, Brandt became chancellor shortly after leftist student uprisings shook neighboring France and while Western European nations increasingly opposed U.S. involvement in the Vietnam War.

would like historians to view him, Brandt replied modestly, "I would be happy if they found that I had done something to make my country a good neighbor in Europe." On December 10 Brandt arrived in Oslo with Rut, to formally accept the prize that he had worked so hard to have presented to Carl Ossietzky in 1935–36. With his Norwegian-born daughter Ninja present, Brandt was greeted as "*vaar egen Willy*" ("our own Willy") by admiring citizens of Norway. The Nobel chairman, who had known Brandt as a young exile in Oslo, commended him for the "attempt to bury hatred."

As Brandt looked from the stage into the vague collection of faces sitting before him in the dark, he remembered the young man he had once been, "persecuted, driven to Norway and deprived of German citizenship." That same person, he said, "is not now speaking solely on behalf of European peace, in general, but also, and more especially, for those from whom the past has exacted a heavy toll."

Looking into the faces of Norwegian and German friends, who years before had stood by him in exile, Brandt continued, "I welcome the privilege after the ineffaceable horrors of the past to bring the name of my country and the desire for peace into accord. Indeed, to reduce the words 'Germany' and 'peace' to a common denominator."

Vice-chancellor and Foreign Minister Brandt formed a "Grand Coalition" with Chancellor Kurt Georg Kiesinger (right) to govern West Germany. Kiesinger, who had served in the Nazi foreign ministry, became troubled by Brandt's successful talks with President Charles de Gaulle of France.

This was a moment of triumph for Brandt. But not everyone involved in the international political scene was happy with his policy of easing tensions with the Eastern Bloc. Among his critics were U.S. National Security Adviser Henry Kissinger, U.S. secretary of defense Melvin Laird, and Assistant Secretary of State for Central European Affairs Martin Hillenbrand — all important cabinet and staff members in the administration of Richard Nixon, who had been elected president in 1968. Dean Acheson, former secretary of state under President Harry Truman and foreign-policy adviser to President Kennedy, called Brandt's foreign policy Ostpolitik a "mad race to Moscow." It would not, however, be these disagreements with the United States that would ruin Brandt's seemingly bright political future. In fact, the Nixon administration would soon approach Soviet leader Leonid Brezhnev to initiate its own Eastern policy, known as détente, aimed at reducing tensions and negotiating the Strategic Arms Limitations Talks (SALT). Rather, it would be deceit and betrayal inside his own government that would bring about the end of his chancellorship.

With his wife, Rut, Brandt receives the Nobel Peace Prize in Oslo, Norway, on December 10, 1971. He won the prize for his orchestration of Ostpolitik, promoting peace between communist and noncommunist nations.

8

Scandal and Resignation

In December 1973 Willy Brandt celebrated his 60th birthday. Forty years after his exile Brandt was recognized by leaders at home and abroad, friend and foe alike, as one of the principal architects of postwar Germany. However, beneath the surface of Brandt's success a political storm was brewing. Despite the sensational foreign-policy achievements, Brandt's domestic initiatives were stymied by strong opposition from the coalition formed by the conservative Christian Democratic Union and the Christian Social Union. Finding themselves unable to derail Ostpolitik, the conservatives stepped up their efforts to deflate Brandt's accomplishments at home. Nevertheless, Brandt's first term as chancellor enjoyed a basically stable and prosperous economy.

Brandt led the Social Democrats to a decisive victory in the national election of 1973 with a hefty 53 percent of the vote. On December 14, 1973, Willy Brandt was formally sworn in for his second term

For four years Willy played God and now he's playing the Crucified.
—HELMUT SCHMIDT Brandt's successor as chancellor, on the Guillaume scandal

Exhausted and disappointed, Brandt attends a meeting in Bonn after Günter Guillaume, a member of his staff, was arrested for espionage on April 24, 1974. Guillaume, an East German spy, had made his way from a minor position in Frankfurt to the innermost chambers of the West German government.

Brandt and his trusted assistant Guillaume, who first became suspect when German counterespionage officers learned he had been an officer in the East German Army. Brandt was informed of Guillaume's spying in May 1973. A year later, Brandt resigned as chancellor in light of the scandal.

as chancellor. As his colleagues rose to applaud their party leader, Günter Guillaume, a minor official within the Social Democratic party, stood unnoticed in the rear of the parliamentary chambers. In the months to come events would push Guillaume from the shadows into center stage with Brandt.

Overt tensions between East and West Germany lessened considerably during Brandt's first term as chancellor. Neither country, however, reduced their ongoing efforts to secretly infiltrate the other's political ranks in order to obtain classified information and influence policy.

Between the two Germanys, espionage in many ways was (and is) easier for two reasons. First, a common native language and similar background allowed spies to operate with less vulnerability to detection. In addition, West Germany welcomed refugees from the East. Thus, inadvertently, red-carpet treatment was given to East Germans who were actually entering the country as spies. In just this way by 1974, Günter Guillaume, a low-level secret agent planted initially in Frankfurt by his East German superiors 17 years before, became well established in the Federal Chancellery as Brandt's liaison for party affairs.

A rather portly middle-aged man with spectacles, Guillaume appeared to be just another member of the government bureaucracy. In the first year of Brandt's second term, Guillaume served on Brandt's personal staff and that summer even accompanied the chancellor and his family on holiday to Norway. Brandt seemed comfortable with Guillaume, able to rely on his ability to oversee necessary but tedious detail work. For a powerful man of politics, such as Brandt, Guillaume seemed the perfect subordinate.

Not everyone within Brandt's administration regarded Guillaume as harmless. Numerous rumors and incriminating bits of information had been surfacing for years, arousing suspicions that this supposed East German refugee was not to be trusted in West German government. Because West German intelligence was slow to act on these pieces of evidence, Brandt remained in the dark concerning Guillaume possibly being a spy for East Germany.

Brandt's resignation as chancellor over the Guillaume spy scandal met with protest from many of his supporters, who believed that he was blameless in the matter and should not be held responsible for having Guillaume in his government.

As president of the Socialist International, Brandt addresses socialist leaders from around the world in 1975. While chancellor of West Germany, he had demonstrated extraordinary understanding in international affairs. In 1976 Brandt was appointed by World Bank president Robert McNamara to head a commission to study developing nations.

Meanwhile, Brandt was confronting important domestic problems as well as a serious challenge from his finance minister and the new deputy chairman of the SPD, Helmut Schmidt, for the leadership of the Social Democratic party. For the first time in many years, Brandt was being forced to play defensive politics. With Ostpolitik now a past achievement, Brandt seemed uninspired by the more mundane domestic and party politics requiring his attention.

Finally, in May 1973, Brandt was privately informed by his minister of the interior, Hans Dietrich Genscher, that there was "more than vague suspicion" that Guillaume was an East German intelligence agent. Generally inclined to think only very highly of the people he worked with, Brandt assumed Guillaume was simply the object of rumors promoted by jealous subordinates who resented Guillaume's position on the chancellor's staff. Brandt could see no reason to suspect Guillaume or question his loyalty. Brandt's unalarmed reaction was relayed to West German intelligence; the seriousness with which the matter was treated began to dissipate.

From time to time Brandt would inquire whether any new evidence had been gathered against Guillaume. The answer was no. In truth, there was no more *additional* evidence. However, what had been gathered was now being ignored. This trend continued until 1974. In the meantime, Guillaume's cover was thick enough to deceive even East German officials unaware of his ongoing intelligence assignment. If Guillaume was aware of any suspicion surrounding himself, he also completely ignored the issue, neither denying nor attempting to discredit what for now was a vague collection of rumors and inconclusive evidence.

A highly suspicious birthday greeting transmitted to Guillaume by East German operatives but intercepted by West German counterintelligence agents finally forced the Federal Office for Protection (the German equivalent to the United States FBI) to act. On April 24, 1974, Guillaume was arrested in his home, where authorities found him packing his luggage and about to flee West Germany.

That afternoon as he arrived at the Bonn airport from an official tour of the Middle East, Brandt was told of Guillaume's arrest. Although he immediately realized his chancellorship was in danger, Brandt did not panic. What seemed to shock him, however, was that he had for the first time been betrayed by a man he had taken completely into his confidence. He returned to the government offices lost in thought.

Guillaume met his interrogators with a determined silence. Twenty hours passed before the government revealed Guillaume's arrest to the public. When the news hit, the political explosion was deaf-

> *I am no plaster saint and never claimed to be free of weaknesses.*
> —WILLY BRANDT

> *I am not going to allow someone to make me shift my policy, which is basically a correct and necessary policy, merely by planting a louse on me.*
>
> —WILLY BRANDT
> prior to resigning

ening. Every major politician in Bonn became fair game for speculations by the press and accusation by political foes. The major prize, however, was Brandt. Gossip and uncertainty ran rampant through the West German capital. The Federal Press Office tried to offset this flood of rumor and misinformation by issuing a statement that Guillaume "was not connected with work on subjects classified as secret." The damage, however, was done.

By the first of May, the West German government had come virtually to a halt. The business of government had given way to countless investigations, each conceived to uncover the truth or, in some cases, the version of the truth that would either end or encourage further speculation.

Initially, Brandt stood firm. He told associates that he had been victimized by overzealous investigators, more interested in his private life than in the background of an admitted spy. But as the conservative opposition's political attacks intensified, Brandt became noticeably tired and nervous. His normally robust features became drawn with worry. By May 4, the possibility of Brandt's resignation could no longer be ignored.

Until the afternoon of May 7, Brandt indicated that he was upset, but planned to stand and fight as chancellor. That evening, however, word was received that Guillaume had indeed seen sensitive NATO documents. This was a charge Brandt felt he could not survive.

On May 7, 1974, Brandt sent the following letter to Federal President Gustav Heinemann:

> "Dear Mr. Federal President: I assume the political responsibility for acts of negligence in connection with the Guillaume affair and declare my resignation from the office of Chancellor . . . effective immediately . . . Yours, Willy Brandt."

It was over. Nearly 18 months after his inauguration for a second term as chancellor, Willy Brandt stepped down. He was succeeded by his Social Democratic rival, Helmut Schmidt, whom Brandt had reluctantly affirmed as being the "first man of the SPD in the cabinet of Willy Brandt."

Two blocks away from the chancellery, a new exhibition was opening. It commemorated the 800-year history of Lübeck. Brandt had been scheduled weeks before to attend as guest of honor by the man who handled his agenda, Günter Guillaume. But Lübeck's favorite son would not be in attendance. Instead, Willy Brandt sent his regrets.

In retrospect, many political analysts feel that Brandt did not have to resign as chancellor. Although this step was to his credit — as it allowed West Germany to put the Guillaume affair aside and resume the more important business of government —it was not strictly necessary.

Rumors persist that Guillaume had actually discovered some dark secret in Brandt's personal life, which he threatened to reveal if the chancellor remained in office. Brandt's weaknesses were well-known, and these offered ample opportunity to those looking to discredit him. But he had successfully weathered past personal attacks. Regardless of whatever information they obtained from Guillaume, the spy's East German superiors had also helped bring down the West German chancellor who had proven the least hostile to the East.

An additional explanation is that Brandt was, in fact, losing heart and interest in the job. Willy Brandt was a master of identifying and understanding the big picture. He loved the opportunities politics afforded him to make the large and dramatic gesture, such as falling to his knees at the Warsaw Memorial, or undertaking the sweeping foreign affairs policy, Ostpolitik. But Brandt, the Nobel Prize winner, the successful campaigner and treaty-maker, the prodigal son welcomed home, the man who could stop an angry mob at the Berlin Wall and extend his hand in peace to his former adversaries, was less interested in the constant provincial political details and minor party disagreements that landed on his desk. He missed the intensity and excitement of Berlin and had never enjoyed living in Bonn. Finally, the constant attacks from conservatives for treating the left wing at home and the communists abroad too gently had, after a decade, left him tired and, ultimately, bored.

Social Democrat Helmut Schmidt succeeded Brandt as chancellor of West Germany in 1974. Schmidt, an economist, had served in such important cabinet posts under Brandt as minister of defense and minister of finance.

Brandt had achieved his major goal of realigning West Germany with the East and its Western allies in a way that could not be reversed. Discounting the scandal, his record was good, his place in history assured. He could hardly hope to improve either by staying on as chancellor. And if the previous year was any clue, he could only damage his already considerable accomplishments. Thus, May 7, 1974 was not an end for Willy Brandt. It was simply a transition.

A much different future faced Günter Guillaume. The East German spy was sentenced to 13 years in prison for espionage. His career was finished. He was out of work and unemployable.

Willy Brandt's career was far from over. Even with the scandal and his resignation still fresh in voters' minds, Helmut Schmidt insisted Brandt remain chairman of the SPD. From this office, the former chancellor was able to keep a low political profile and take some much needed time for rest and reflection.

Much to Schmidt's dismay, however, resignation did not temper Brandt's distaste for some of his successor's ideas of social democracy. As chairman of the Social Democrats, Brandt often appeared to deny Schmidt his allegiance by allowing the young leftists within the party to speak up against Chancellor Schmidt's more centrist, mainstream positions. Nevertheless, in 1975 both Brandt and Schmidt were reelected to their positions of chairman of the SPD and chancellor of the Federal Republic.

With the scandal fading into history, numerous international posts were soon rumored to be offered to Brandt, including UN secretary general and a high position in the European Common Market. Neither materialized. Instead, in 1976, Brandt was elected president of the Socialist International, a world alliance of socialist governments. Later that same year he was named chairman of the Independent Commission on International Development Issues by World Bank president and former U.S. secretary of defense Robert McNamara. Brandt welcomed the offer. As chairman of such a prestigious international body, he could refurbish his image in German and European politics, and once again have the opportunity to act upon the world political stage.

The Brandt Commission, as this agency came to be known, was established to research and offer possible solutions to the political and economic problems between the industrialized world and developing nations. In 1980 the Brandt Commission presented a controversial report, outlining a worldwide emergency program of increased developmental aid, energy cooperation, food production, and economic reform that is still being debated today.

No people can live without pride. This is as true for Germany as it is for other people.
—WILLY BRANDT

Brandt's personal life continued to capture as much attention as his political ideas. In 1978 he suffered a severe heart attack that, as he described it, "brought him to the border of life and death." The following year he announced his intention to divorce his wife in order to continue his relationship with Brigitte Seebacker, a 32-year-old political assistant. Many Germans were saddened by the breakup of Brandt's 30-year marriage, but not terribly surprised. Rut had stood at Brandt's side through many personal and political crises, including his occasional affairs with other women. Nevertheless, Brandt was not dismayed by any negative public reaction and continued his work with the SPD, the Socialist International, and the Brandt Commission with the vigor of a man 20 years his junior. In 1987, at the age of 74, Willy Brandt continues his quest for peace, actively spurring the moral conscience of the world with his visions of mutual development and peace among nations, friend and foe alike.

Brandt and his second wife, Brigitte Seebecker, in December 1983. He divorced his Norwegian-born wife of 30 years, Rut, in order to marry his 32-year-old political assistant.

"I have always believed that the common sense of the majority will ultimately triumph over the ideological and political extremists who criticize rational arrangements for international stability as hopeless utopianism or moral cowardice," Brandt wrote in the late 1980s, giving evidence that neither age nor the continued march of history had weakened his convictions. Looking more fit and cheerful than he did more than a decade earlier while facing political scandal and defeat, Brandt told friends, "I am determined to live as I want for the few years ahead of me."

In June 1987 Willy Brandt stepped down as official chairman of the Social Democrats at a convention of the party's parliamentary group in Bonn. He was succeeded by Hans Jochen Vogel, a former mayor of Munich, and a supporter of Brandt during the heyday of Ostpolitik. Brandt retained the position of honorary chairman. Still keenly aware of the adversities confronting both the Third World and the possibilities for greater international cooperation, Brandt wrote that year: "That the political unification is progressing so slowly is another story. It results not only from incompetence on the part of governments but also from the inescapable burden that comes with the history of nation states."

Brandt, at age 73, tapes a television interview near the Brandenburg Gate in Berlin in 1986. In June 1987 he stepped down as chairman of the Social Democratic party. He was succeeded by Hans Jochen Vogel.

Further Reading

Balfour, Michael. *West Germany: A Contemporary History*. New York: St. Martin's Press, 1982.

Binder, David. *The Other German—Willy Brandt's Life and Times*. Washington, D.C.: The New Republic Book Company, 1975.

Brandt, Willy. *In Exile—Essays, Reflections and Letters*. Philadelphia: University of Pennsylvania Press, 1971.

Brandt, Willy. *My Road to Berlin*. Garden City, NY: Doubleday, 1960.

Brandt, Willy. *People and Politics: The Years 1960–1975*. Boston: Little, Brown, 1976.

Brandt, Willy. *The Ordeal of Coexistence*. Cambridge, MA: Harvard University Press, 1963.

Drath, Viola Herms. *Willy Brandt—Prisoner of his Past*. Radnor, PA: Chilton, 1975.

Manchester, William. *The Glory and the Dream—A Narrative History of America: 1932–1972*. Boston: Little, Brown, 1973.

Chronology

Dec. 18, 1913	Herbert Ernst Karl Frahm born in Lübeck, Germany
Aug. 1914	Archduke Franz Ferdinand of Austria is assassinated; World War I begins
June 1919	Treaty of Versailles
May 6, 1930	Frahm writes a controversial article and fends off hostile reactions by means of his first attempt to change his name to "Willy Brandt"
Sept. 14, 1930	Reichstag elections make the Nazis the second most powerful political group in Germany, at the expense of the Social Democrats
Jan. 30, 1933	Adolf Hitler appointed chancellor of the Weimar republic
Feb. 23, 1933	Fire (suspected arson) in the Reichstag building; further weakening of the power of the German government
March 23, 1933	Reichstag passes the "Enabling Act," making Hitler dictator
March 31, 1933	Frahm flees Germany for Norway
1933	Appointed head of Norwegian Refugee Federation
Sept. 3, 1938	Frahm's German citizenship is revoked
Sept. 1, 1939	Germany invades Poland; World War II begins
April 9, 1940	Germany invades Norway
	Frahm flees Norway for Sweden
1942	Writes *Guerillakriget*
May 8, 1945	Germany surrenders to Allied forces
May 10, 1945	Frahm leaves Stockholm for Oslo with his wife, Carlota
1946	Covers the Nuremberg trials as a Norwegian correspondent
1948	Becomes executive representative in Berlin for Chairman Schumacher of the Social Democratic party
1949	Legally changes his name to "Willy Brandt"
1950–1957	Serves as special assistant to West Berlin's mayor Ernst Reuter
Nov. 1956	Pacifies Soviet army and anti-Soviet rebels in Berlin
1957–1966	Serves as mayor of West Berlin
1963	Loses election for chancellor of Germany to Ludwig Erhard
1969	Elected chancellor
1971	Named *Time*'s "Man of the Year"; Awarded Nobel Peace Prize
1973	Begins second term as chancellor
1974	Günter Guillaume becomes Brandt's liaison for party affairs
April 24, 1974	Guillaume arrested as East German spy
May 7, 1974	Brandt resigns his position as chancellor
1976	Elected president of Socialist International
	Named head of Independent Commission on International Development Issues (the Brandt Commission)

Index

Tom Viola specializes in arts, entertainment, and communications fields. His work has appeared in many national magazines. A former actor, he lives in Manhattan.

Arthur M. Schlesinger, jr., taught history at Harvard for many years and is currently Albert Schweitzer Professor of the Humanities at City University of New York. He is the author of numerous highly praised works in American history and has twice been awarded the Pulitzer Prize. He served in the White House as special assistant to Presidents Kennedy and Johnson.